W9-CXY-576

THE
LOFTIER
WAY

Books by Blaine M. Yorgason and/or Brenton G. Yorgason

The Loftier Way: Tales from the Ancient American Frontier
Brother Brigham's Gold
Ride the Laughing Wind
The Miracle
Chester, I Love You
Double Exposure
Seeker of the Gentle Heart
The Krystal Promise
A Town Called Charity and Other Stories about Decisions
The Bishop's Horse Race
The Courage Covenant (Massacre at Salt Creek)
Windwalker (movie version—out of print)
The Windwalker
Others
Charlie's Monument
From First Date to Chosen Mate
Tall Timber (out of print)
Miracles and the Latter-day Saint Teenager (out of print)
*From Two to One**
*From This Day Forth**
Creating a Celestial Marriage (textbook)*
Marriage and Family Stewardships (textbook)*

Tapes

Caring and Sharing (Blaine M. Yorgason—two taped talks)
Things Most Plain and Precious (Brenton G. Yorgason—
    two taped talks)
The Joyous Way (Blaine and Brenton Yorgason—two taped talks)
The Miracle (dramatized tape of book)
Charlie's Monument (taped reading of book)
The Bishop's Horse Race (taped reading of book)

*Coauthored with Wesley R. Burr and Terry R. Baker

THE
LOFTIER
WAY

Tales from the
Ancient American Frontier

Blaine and Brenton
YORGASON

Deseret Book

Salt Lake City, Utah

©1985 Deseret Book Company
All rights reserved
Printed in the United States of America

No part of this book may be reproduced in any
form or by any means without permission in writing
from the publisher, Deseret Book Company,
P.O. Box 30178, Salt Lake City, Utah 84130.

ISBN 0-87747-785-X
Library of Congress Catalog Number 85-70919

First printing May 1985

*For teachers of the gospel everywhere,
who have the overwhelming responsibility
of showing others how to see.*

Contents

Preface

The prophet Nephi stated that he likened the scriptures to his people for their profit and learning. (1 Nephi 19:23.) As seminary teachers we quickly discovered that not much had changed in the centuries since Nephi had made his statement. The young people we were teaching seemed to better understand the scriptures when we showed them that ancient events were similar to events we experience today, and when we showed them too that people had not changed much over the years.

Because we are by nature tellers of stories, we found that we too better understood the concepts and doctrines taught in the scriptures when we made tales of them. Thus we soon found ourselves reading between the lines, thinking of the people who took part in the events described, wondering about their emotions and activities and struggles, and subconsciously forming these wonderments into tales. These were always fictitious, for in them we placed our own thoughts, feelings, struggles, and testimonies.

The following nine stories, with their discovery notes explaining the wheres and whys of our ideas, reflect lessons and doctrines that the scriptural accounts in the Book of Mormon have helped us to understand. None is official doctrine of The Church of Jesus Christ of Latter-

day Saints, none takes into account or is meant to reflect
any culture or thought pattern other than our own, and
we take sole responsibility for all statements in this volume. Nor is this small book meant in any way to take the
place of the scriptures, the Lord's word to us. In searching them only do we have the promise of eternal life.

Still, as we have read the Book of Mormon, studied,
pondered, gained some understanding, and, finally,
written, we have felt a spirit of love for the ancient
peoples of the Lord. We truly pray that those who read
these stories may feel the same spirit and understand a
little more clearly the next time they read the scriptures
themselves.

Acknowledgments

We express our gratitude to Doris Barkdull, who shared a very personal journal entry that led to the story "The Woman."

Introduction

Centuries before the westering Europeans came to the shores of frontier America, this great land, both north and south of the equator, was a frontier in many ways for other people, other ways of life.

We don't know exactly what the country was like those long millenniums past, but it is not difficult to imagine. Then, as now, it must have been a land of challenge, of great difficulty, and of unbelievable beauty. In places the grass would have been as high as a tall man's head; in others the trees would have been so thick that a man might walk for miles without ever seeing sky. The deserts, undeveloped, would have been even more harsh than they are today, and the jungles would have been even more dark, mysterious, and impenetrable. In early spring the meadows would have been abloom with flowers; in winter the harshness of the season would have taught the value of snug shelters. Yet the earth was rich for the growing of crops, and there was game aplenty to keep a family alive until such crops might be harvested.

The plains and the deserts must have seemed without limits, the mountains and the forests unending, and so people must have felt the same about themselves. Anything was possible, and thus great things were accomplished. Trails were made and men took them eagerly, roads were built up, homes were established, and in the

1

process, horizons were expanded and men grew even more.

Where they walked on the land there was opportunity, and when they rested there was anticipation. Often in their growth they made mistakes, but progress is sometimes built upon a foundation of error, and the progress of those ancient people led to the formation of great civilizations.

Then, as now, this was no land for the faint of heart or weak in spirit. Instead, it was a land for men and women to grow in, a frontier filled always with new horizons. In the conquering of these horizons, one day and one challenge at a time, these people gained the strength and courage to tackle the even greater frontiers of the mind and spirit, the loftier and often more lonely way of life.

In the stories that follow, it is this last frontier, the frontier of the spirit, that we have considered. We hope, as you consider this loftier way, that you enjoy reading of what might have been.

The Division

Slowly the man lowered his hand, pushed his writing away, and rubbed at his aching eyes. He was a big man, tall and powerful through the arms and shoulders, wolf-lean through the waist and hips, and supported by muscular legs that drove like pistons whenever he moved.

His face, rock-hard and angular, was at the same time curiously gentle. His deep-set eyes, buried closely against a nose as horn-sharp as an eagle's beak, now stared without seeing. His lips were compressed into a tight thin line, and his hands, coarse from much labor, were clenched tightly at his sides.

To the west the sun moved toward the purple mountains, and as it dropped it gilded the clouds above it with gold, turning the heavens the color of fire. From the trees above him a flock of birds suddenly exploded and screeched away. The grass waved and grew still as a wandering breeze passed by, and the man remained silent, staring ahead.

In his mind echoed the words of the men and women he had confronted; their words, their threats, their laughter and their mockery. Over and over he rehearsed the scene in his mind, and with each repetition he felt once more his bafflement at their lack of understanding, his fear for their eternal well-being, his total frustration at their continued hatred, and, above all else, his great

3

anguish over his own weakness, the weakness that seemed to have contributed so to their wickedness.

Now, with his heart sorrowing over his loss of control, his mind rehearsed the responses he had made to them and concocted others that would have been better.

He thought then of his father, so recently dead, of the things the elderly man might have said, and in loneliness his heart cried out across the great gulf of immortality. "Oh my father," he moaned softly, "if only you were here. I feel so alone, and the words they utter strike like arrows at my soul. Nor do I blame them, for my words too have become harsh and filled with anger. Yea, I am filled with weakness because of my flesh.

"Yet their lies twist at me, cutting like a knife, and their consuming hatred ravages my reason until I react with anger as evil as their own! Oh, if only—"

Slowly the man stood and made his way to the small stream. There he stared at the water that chuckled and hurried along before him. Reaching down, he took up a stone and tossed it aimlessly, watching the small splash and listening as the sound of the rock striking the bottom echoed back hollowly.

Shortly he picked up a second stone and threw it, and then another and another; and while he was doing that, he heard the step behind him and felt the firm but gentle pressure of a hand on his shoulder.

Turning, he gazed down into the face of his wife, the daughter of his mother's brother, the one whom the Lord had given him to wed. Instantly he noted the concern in her deep green eyes, and immediately he turned away, not wanting her to see his weakness.

The lovely young woman smiled, stepped around in front of him, and pecked him on his gaunt and whiskered cheek.

"Your wife greets you," she said softly.

"Your husband greets you in return," the man replied uneasily.

"May I join you?"

"Are you certain that you wish to do so?"

The woman, taking hold of her husband's big hand, responded quickly. "Of course! Were we not counseled to share our ways and our thoughts? My husband, I would share yours."

"And my weaknesses as well?" he asked bitterly.

"Even those," the woman replied seriously. "Now may I join you?"

The man nodded slightly, squeezed her hand, and then stared once more at the stream.

"Them again?" she asked softly after a long moment of silence.

Again the man nodded.

"This time it must have been much worse," the woman observed as she pressed to share her husband's emotional burden. "I have not seen it do this to you before."

"It *was* worse," the big man replied, almost whispering. "I made it so, for when I finished, they threatened even you and the children. Never have they spoken with such hatred as they did when I declared the word of the Lord to them! And now I fear for what I have done."

The woman's face showed her skepticism. She knew this man, knew his heart, knew of his closeness to his God, and so she doubted.

The man, his emotions at last bursting forth, did not see her doubt, but he continued. "Father had such a way with them. Perhaps he loved them more than I do. Perhaps he was simply a better man. I don't know. But his patience, his long-suffering, was *boundless*.

"Mine, on the other hand, is . . . is . . ."

The man looked briefly into the still but expectant face of his wife, turned, picked up another stone, and threw it forcefully into the stream.

"Mine," he continued bitterly, "is nonexistent!"

The woman dropped her eyes and thought long and carefully before at last she spoke.

"Will you tell me of their words?" she finally asked.

"I would rather not," the man replied bleakly. "They were the same words as always. Worse, however, was my response, for when I should have shown forth love and understanding, my heart spewed forth anger, so much so that their own wrath burned even more brightly."

"So with their cruelty they brought forth your anger," the woman summarized.

Sadly the man nodded, his features transparently showing the frustration and sorrow that was within him.

"Yes," he whispered, "and they did it quickly, almost without effort, and *gleefully*."

"Of course they were gleeful," the woman responded. "Don't they always delight in their efforts to make you less than you are?"

"Yes," the man answered, "they seem to. But—"

"But," the woman continued, interrupting him, "that isn't really the problem at all. The problem is that this will be the last time, won't it? The Lord has commanded you to leave them."

Quickly the man turned and looked at his wife.

"You know?" he asked in surprise.

"I have known since early this morning," she answered quietly.

"But how . . ."

"By the whisperings of the Spirit, my husband. Still, all this day have I doubted and hoped that it would not be so. It was not until I saw you that I was certain."

"My wife, I have said nothing—"

"Of course you haven't. But I know you very well, perhaps even better than you know yourself. That is why you have come to this place, which you have avoided completely since your father's passing. Here is where he felt closest to the Lord, and here you feel the same."

Again the man looked deeply into the face of his wife. "Tell me," he asked gently as he took hold of her shoulders, "what else is there that you see? What else is there that you know by the voice of the Spirit?"

The woman smiled and without hesitation responded. "I know of your great self-reproach, and I sorrow because of it. My husband, you have the idea that you should be above such emotions as anger. You wrongly feel that your anger has contributed to their downfall, and you feel, wrongly still, that if you had not spoken so harshly, you would never have been commanded to flee from their wrath."

For a moment the man was still, gazing down into the face of his wife. Finally he turned and stared off into the trees.

"I do feel those things, and I am afraid I am not wrong. Father would have handled it so differently."

"Perhaps," the woman responded. "But then again, he might have done exactly as you did. Who can know? Yes, you were angry with them, and yes, for you that is not good. But remember, it is easy for anger to mushroom out of love, out of sincere caring, especially when great hatred or stupidity is being shown by the ones we love and care about."

"Truly," the man stated as he turned back to look at his wife, "the Lord has blessed you with great understanding. And you are right. It *was* easy for me to anger, and that is why my heart is filled with pain. I am troubled because the Lord has called me to a high and holy calling, and I am an unworthy servant!

"He has shown me such great things that I am not able even to describe them. He has filled me with His Spirit, even to the consuming of my flesh. Time and again He has protected me from my enemies. And many more times has He blessed me. Yet despite that, I continue to do wrong! I continue to show anger! I ache because I feel that in my weakness I have driven them even further from the truth that I was commissioned to teach them."

"My dear husband," the woman reprimanded gently, "you must remember that you cannot deprive them of their agency. You can teach with all your heart, but God will never allow you to force them to listen. That is contrary to His way."

"Is it His way to call a weak man to be His prophet?"

"You are not weak! You are only human, and a very special one at that."

Again the man looked at his wife. Then he stepped silently to the bank of the tumbling stream. His head bent, and tears started freely from his eyes.

Quickly the woman went to him and placed her hand on his arm. But, wisely, she remained silent.

"It is as you say," the man finally murmured. "I am human, far too human to be what the Lord has asked me to be. Because of my weakness I cannot do it! I, I who have been called to lead my brothers with long-suffering back to God, am quick to anger, quick to take offense. And being so, I but drive them further away.

"Of all men I have been most blessed. Yet still my flesh is weak. I am filled with iniquity because of my anger, I am commanded to flee for my own safety because of my weakness, and my heart cries out to my Lord and my God, 'Help my brothers, please, for wretched man that I am, I cannot!'"

"And that," the woman said softly as she reached up and brushed the tears from her husband's face, "is precisely why the Lord did call you; why you are *not* a wicked man. In all things, do you not seek your God? In all your trials, do you not turn to His word? In your weaknesses, do you not seek His strength?

"You do, my husband. Truly does God know that you are but a man filled with the frailties of the flesh. Yet still He loves you, and He has called you to this high and holy calling because *you* know it and desire with all your heart to rise above it. And that is also why I love you.

"Now I must go, for the children and I must prepare for the journey. Trust in the Lord as you always have, my husband. Remember that His reasons for protecting the righteous are high, even to the preventing of nations yet unborn from dwindling in unbelief. And remember too that even this great trial will turn to the good, not only for you and me and those who do their best to stand firm, but for those who have turned their hearts against God as well."

The man looked down at his lovely wife, the beginnings of a smile playing at the corners of his mouth. "Those words have a very familiar sound, my wife."

The woman smiled in return. "A great and righteous man once taught them to me, a man whom I love more than I love life itself."

Touching the face of his wife gently with his rough hand, the big man softly expressed his gratitude for her ever-present wisdom and strength. Then he watched silently as she climbed the rocks to the rim of the quickly darkening canyon.

At the top his wife smiled and waved, and as she disappeared the man fell quickly to his knees. His heart still ached, his broad shoulders were still bowed with guilt and shame, and his soul wept because the Lord had commanded him to separate himself and his family from those he truly loved. Yet as he poured out his soul to God, he was filled with the beginnings of peace.

Finally, with his heart salved, the man who was called Nephi arose and sat upon the rock before the old stump. Carefully he pulled toward him the small gold plates, the ones upon which he had been writing the things of his soul.

For a time then he read, feeling the sweet spirit of the things he had recorded, remembering the reality of his experiences with the Lord, and remembering too his father and mother and now his wife, loving them the more for the way of righteousness they had shown him, the lonely way that was nevertheless the loftier way of eternal life.

Truly his heart ached for his brethren, but the Spirit whispered, as it had to his father before him, that they would be held accountable only for their own weaknesses and not for his own. His weaknesses were for him alone to grapple with, and, with the Lord's help, he would overcome, he would grow until he had become the man he was expected to be.

Awake, my soul! he inscribed while his heart sang with renewed determination and conviction. *No longer droop in sin. Do not anger again because of mine enemies. Rejoice, O my heart, and cry unto the Lord, and say, O Lord, I will praise thee forever; yea, my soul will rejoice in thee, my God, and the rock of my salvation.*

O Lord, I have trusted in thee, and I will trust in thee forever.

Behold, my voice shall forever ascend up unto thee, my rock and mine everlasting God—

From the Book of 2 Nephi we discover that . . .

Of all the people in the Book of Mormon, the prophet Nephi is perhaps best known. His writings, taken from what he called his small plates,[1] begin the record as we know it today and make up a little over one fifth of the book's total length.[2] In them Nephi presents fascinating word pictures not only of himself, but also of his entire family. In fact, so much information is given in the Book of Mormon about this group of people that this note must, of necessity, limit itself to Nephi's relationship to his family and to the experience portrayed in the preceding story.

Nephi was the fourth of six sons of the prophet Lehi and his wife Sariah. His older brothers were Laman, Lemuel, and Sam, and his younger brothers were Jacob and Joseph.[3] He also had two or more sisters, though their names are not given in our record.[4]

The family left Jerusalem about 600 B.C.,[5] traveled nine or ten years[6] through an uncharted wilderness toward the sea, built a ship there,[7] and, in a voyage that lasted about a year,[8] sailed to a land that they called the Land of Promise,[9] which we today call the Americas.

During that journey Nephi married his cousin, one of the daughters of Ishmael, who was his mother's brother.[10] To this union were born children,[11] but both their gender and their number are unknown.

There is evidence from the beginning of Nephi's record of much hostility between himself and his two eldest brothers,[12] and this hostility increased when Nephi determined to strictly follow his father and the Lord.[13] Sam agreed immediately to follow Nephi's decision and direction,[14] but Laman and

Lemuel hardened their hearts,[15] and with only occasional exceptions[16] this animosity increased as the years passed.

Very quickly the hostility reached murderous proportions,[17] brought about by dissatisfaction among some of the sons and daughters of Ishmael, among whom were the wives of Laman and Lemuel.[18] From then on Nephi's life was one continual round of calling his brothers to repentance, being placed by them in life-threatening situations, and then being rescued and preserved by the intervention of the Lord.[19] These events culminated following Lehi's death when the final conflict occurred that led to the preceding story and to Nephi's decision, made under divine direction, to separate himself and his people from his two eldest brothers and those who were following them.[20]

Concerning this final conflict, Nephi gives us the following specifics:

First, his brothers were angry because he had preached (the truth) to them. For that they had determined irrevocably to take his life.[21]

Second, the conflict occurred "not many days" after Lehi's death.[22] Nephi had not "ruled" long at all, but it is obvious that it was more than too long for Laman and Lemuel.

Third, the conflict occurred for precisely this reason. The older brothers were angry and jealous because the Lord had given the younger brother jurisdiction over them, and their pride would not allow them to accept that and live with it.[23]

Fourth, and finally, the incident caused Nephi to begin considering his brothers as his "enemies."[24]

Beyond this specific information, some other things are stated ambiguously or implied. Apparently the affair, with all of its ramifications, was so unpleasant to Nephi that he anguished over it to the Lord, wrote down his feelings about it as well as the part he played in it, and so left us the inspired prayer known today as Nephi's Psalm.[25]

Many in modern times have read Nephi's writings and have grown discouraged over them, anguishing because Nephi seems so much more than human. This poetic psalm should help all of us to see how very human he was, for in it he honestly reveals his weakness, at least a part of the reason for his great despair.

When Laman and Lemuel turned on their brother, Nephi reacted with anger against their wickedness.[26] His was not the long-suffering attitude of his father nor the way of patience taught by the scriptures he so loved to study. It was debasing anger, perhaps loud, perhaps physical, but, at the very least, out of control. Nephi considered this a sin,[27] and in his prayer he revealed that he was striving through soul-searching repentance for the loftier way he knew was right.

Obviously the way he was seeking was also the lonely way, for as he took it he left many of those he loved behind, left them wallowing in the broad path of sin and self-pity and pride that would lead them, ultimately, to their own destruction.

In the story only a small portion of the prayer is recorded. The reader would be well advised to read all of it just as Nephi recorded it in chapter 4 of Second Nephi.

---

1. 1 Nephi 9:2,6; 19:3-4; 2 Nephi 4:15.
2. The small plates of Nephi included the books First and Second Nephi, Jacob, Enos, Jarom, and Omni, some 132 of the total 522 pages of the Book of Mormon. Mormon, in the Words of Mormon, verses 3 through 7, gives an interesting picture of these plates that is well worth reading.
3. 2 Nephi 5:6.
4. Ibid.
5. 1 Nephi 1, footnote.
6. 1 Nephi 18, footnote.
7. 1 Nephi 18:1-4.
8. 1 Nephi 18:23, footnote.
9. 1 Nephi 18:23-25.
10. Lucy Mack Smith letter, *Ensign*, October 1982, pp. 70-73. This information was apparently recorded in the 116 pages of manuscript called the Book of Lehi, which was translated by Joseph Smith and subsequently lost by Martin Harris.
11. 2 Nephi 5:14.
12. 1 Nephi 2:11.
13. 1 Nephi 2:16-24; 3:7; 16:22-23.
14. 1 Nephi 2:17.
15. 1 Nephi 2:18; 16:32.
16. 1 Nephi 16:5.
17. 1 Nephi 16:37.
18. Ibid.
19. 1 Nephi 16:37-39; 17:48-55; 18:10-21.
20. 2 Nephi 5:2-7.
21. 2 Nephi 5:3-4.
22. 2 Nephi 4:13.
23. 1 Nephi 3:29; 2 Nephi 5:2-4.
24. 2 Nephi 4:22, 27, 29.
25. 2 Nephi 4:15-35.
26. 2 Nephi 4:27, 29.
27. 2 Nephi 4:17-19.

The Mother

As long as I live, even through all the unknown vistas of my upcoming eternity, I will never forget this day. Yet it began ordinarily enough, a day of lonely beauty during which I did the things I have always done and thought through the memories that lived with me always.

When word first came, word which I almost dared not believe, noon's great brightness had left the river and the plain in cooling shadow. But still the day spread and glowed over the yet undimmed mountains to the west. These lifted their lofty peaks pale and sharp through the high, silent air, while deep down between the blue gashes of their canyons the sun threw long shafts of yellow light, indiscriminately splashing them with beauty on their lower slopes. The glazed abodes of the mountain's snow-fields shown separate and clear upon their lofty vastness, pale blue in the shadows, and more white than white where the sun yet kissed their icy faces.

Opposite them, up the valley and far more distant, rose another range of mountains, the coastal range, not sharp, but long and ample. These were bare in some high places, and below these bare ribs of the mountains, trees stretched everywhere, high and low, colored with every shade of green, a world of serene undulations, a great sweet country of silence. It was from the direction of these latter hills that word first reached me.

13

The runner was alone. He traveled with great haste, and the word he carried was so staggering and incredible that my old mind could hardly grasp it. Long I stood after he had gone, watching where the dust from his passing had settled, wondering.

Could it be? After such a long time, was it really possible?

The gradually dying day mounted further up the hills. Warm air eddied slowly in its wake, the scents of the afternoon stirred together and became heavy with sweetness, and still I could not move. I could only think, remembering my old memories more vividly than ever.

Fourteen years! Fourteen long years had they been gone. And I, old and bent with the cares and worries of the world, had long since reconciled myself to the fact that I would see them again only in eternity.

Nor did that thought embitter me. I had taught them as children to serve their God, and once they had finally decided to do so, it was hardly my place to complain. In fact, I was thrilled with their great faith, and along with their father I rejoiced in their determination to serve.

Yet, in spite of that, there has not been a day in all of those fourteen years that my heart has not yearned and my soul cried out in loneliness and fear for those four of my sons. I gave them life and loved them as only a mother can love, and as only a mother can miss a child I have missed them. Then too, they went forth among our enemies, and each day in my heart I have seen, motherlike, the pain and the suffering they must surely be enduring.

Thus, as the singing of the multicolored birds in the forest behind my home became the melancholy sound of another lonely night approaching, I wondered.

And now, even now, as the small things of the night chirp and whir beyond my window, and as I labor to see and to write in the flickering of my single candle, the tears start again and my old heart pounds until I worry that it will awaken them all.

Truly do I rejoice, and truly do I marvel at the goodness and the mercy of my God. He has heard the yearnings of my heart, the unspoken prayers of my soul, and in his infinite mercy has he brought my sons, my four loyal and righteous sons, once more to my hearth.

O that I could dance and leap and sing, so great is my joy! O that my old and withered limbs had the strength! Yet my heart soars higher than the lofty peaks I watch each day, and that is enough, that is enough.

I ache that their father Mosiah no longer lives. How I would rejoice if I could share this day with him. He was so proud of them, so proud of their strength and courage. How he loved to spend his days with them and with their brothers and sisters as well, out in the mountains or in our home, laughing, playing, teaching, or just sitting silently with them. He was such a good father, and even when the duties of his office took so much of his time he did his best to give himself to them.

I'll not forget his agony as these four chose to turn against all the things we'd taught, all the truths we'd espoused. Long we prayed and endlessly, days we fasted, and yet it seemed that the more we did the further away these sons of ours were driven. I wept continuously, my husband took long walks alone, we prayed constantly, and we discussed it endlessly with our good friend Alma, whose son had also chosen the foolish way. But never was there an answer. In nothing could we find the means of turning their hearts away from their wickedness and evil.

And then came the day, years after we had begun praying, when the Lord answered our prayers and the prayers of our friends, and from that day all things changed. No longer did we weep in sorrow but in rejoicing. Our sons were home once more, their hearts and spirits were pure, and we could see that each was studiously endeavoring to keep all of God's commandments.

Nor will I forget the day they came to us requesting permission to go up to the land of Nephi to declare the word of God to our enemies the Lamanites. My poor heart shrank with fear, for I knew of the atrocities committed by the Lamanites upon such of our people as they could capture. Oh, how could my beloved sons desire such a dangerous way of serving the Lord? My husband had refused them, of course, but our sons were adamant, and despite our pleadings and our prayers they persisted in their request.

For many days all we heard was their desire to serve the Lord in the land of Nephi. Finally my husband, good and righteous man that he was, went out and bowed himself down upon the earth in humble and mighty prayer. And the Lord, in his mercy, answered him thus:

Let them go up, for many shall believe on their words, and they shall have eternal life; and I will deliver thy sons out of the hands of the Lamanites.

Now I ask, how can one heart ache with pain and rejoice with pride all at the same time? I know not, yet mine did that day. I thrilled in their righteous desires and in the promise of the Lord that they would not be harmed. Yet I also wept with loneliness already felt because of their coming absence, which I felt even then would last for the remainder of my life.

Still, with our blessings they departed, Ammon the eldest and the shortest in stature, Aaron with the brilliant mind and flash-fire temper, Omner the strong and mostly silent supporter of his brothers, and Himni the youngest, with the sweetest spirit and tenderest heart in all the earth. These and a few choice friends made their way up toward the land of Nephi, leaving me to know they would not come into my life again until forever.

And so for these fourteen long years I have hoped and prayed that they would return. But even more, I have prayed without ceasing that these my sons would continue to be blessed of the Lord in their labors and that I would be able to endure their absence through the remainder of my mortality.

Often have I wished to go to them, to be with them, and, motherlike, to help them bear the terrible trials that I knew they were having. Yet I could not, for it was not the way, and I knew it.

As often too I have wished to send them sustenance, lest they go naked and starving in a far-off land. Yet there was no way that I could do so. My only recourse, then, has been prayer, and as smoke rises to heaven so too have my hourly pleadings, beseeching the Lord that he would succor my sons and take care of their mortal needs.

And this my God has done, praise to His Holy Name, preserving their lives and keeping them for me until this day when the runner came and my old heart leaped with joy and hope.

Thus later, when the sun was gilding only the highest of the distant peaks, the four of them, my four strong and lovely sons, came down the path to my doorway and swept their ancient and feeble mother into their arms, giving me my first true happiness in all these long years.

Oh, to be able to describe my joy, my pride, my gratitude to the Lord! Yet I cannot, for I am but a mortal woman, and such things as I feel within my breast belong only to eternity. Yet how I love my God! With all my heart I love him, for even now, after all this time, he has brought my sons—my sons.

For hours we have talked, the five of us, and I thrill to hear of their successes and their blessings. They have already been with Alma, who is now the Prophet, and the people they brought with them are settled this day in the land of Jershon. Truly my sons' blessings have been many.

I notice, however, that they say little concerning trials and privations. This causes me concern, for I have heard what evil the Lamanites can do, and I shudder to think of what my sons, with their gentle concern and godlike dignity, are hiding from me.

Ammon speaks the most, as he always has, and his humor has developed much over the years. Aaron is not far behind, and he too has a rare wit. Omner, who seems to have aged more than the others (though all seem so much older to me), is mostly silent as his eyes relive each experience his brothers share. And Himni, my youngest and the child of my old age, says nothing, but watches me and glows with the joy of . . . of being home. And though he says nothing, I have always known his heart, and my own goes out to him for the compassion he feels for me, his old and feeble mother. But enough of that, for all are dear to me, none more so than any other, and I rejoice in the presence of each.

They tell me that I could never count the number of converted Lamanites who have accompanied them here; as many, it seems, as the tears I have shed these fourteen years. Again I wonder—I wonder.

Oh they are *home*, my sons are home! My heart cries with joy and rejoicing, and my soul sings with praise to my Lord and my God that I can know them once more.

As we talked, their faces glowed until they seemed radiant with righteousness, and my old heart wonders at the great and marvelous things they have known and seen. It is apparent that they have fasted and prayed much, and they have searched the scriptures until they have developed a sound understanding of the ways and the words of the Lord. But more than that, they seem filled with the spirit of prophecy and revelation, so much so, in fact, that their spirituality and serenity is a vivid thing that spreads to all around them, myself included.

And so I rejoice at the good they have done, and I wonder, will I ever know all of it? Will I ever know the price they must have paid to accomplish such great good? Will I ever understand the miles they have trodden, the hunger they have known, the pain they have suffered, the cruelty they have endured at the hands of those who have for so long been our enemies?

I gathered my courage earlier and asked them of this, and Omner, the strong and silent one, told me only that at first they had feared, but then they had fasted and prayed and the Lord had told them to be comforted. Ammon, with the humor that I have mentioned, added that the Lord had also told them to be patient in affliction that they might be examples, and this he says they have been given ample opportunity to do.

Beyond that they will tell me nothing, and I am left with my fears and with my mother's pain for their suffering, which seems to grow greater the more I think of it. To push these worrisome feelings aside I try to think of the lives they have touched, the testimonies they have borne, the spirits they have sent soaring in righteousness because they have cared enough to serve. But even with that my thoughts keep going back to their sufferings, and I ache for them. Oh that I could have been with them, to ease their suffering, their sorrows . . .

Moments ago, long after all were asleep, I stole among them and gazed long upon their countenances. First Omner, then Ammon and Aaron, and finally Himni. For long moments I stood near my baby and studied his features, thin to gauntness, relaxed in repose, and so familiar yet so strange to me. Standing there looking upon him, I felt such tender feelings as only the mother of a youngest child can know, and my poor old heart ached within me.

What had he gone through, I wondered? What had he endured that he might be a messenger for God? Thus wondering, my imagination again ran wild, and in my mind I could see him clearly, suffering, in torment, starving, thirsting, tortured almost unto death.

"It is enough," I cried in silent prayer. "Let me not think of these things. Let me not learn of their sufferings at the hands of the cruel Lamanites until I am stronger, more able to bear them. Let me think only of the good they have done, the righteousness they have brought to pass."

Hurriedly I turned to leave, but for some reason I stopped and picked up Himni's shoes. They told the story. Worn through again and again, patched over and over, even now the soles were merely rims around the holes through which his feet had pushed painfully against the earth.

Miles and miles of walking he had done, door to door among the Lamanites, thinking not of himself but of them, suffering silently that they might know the message of his God. Oh, if those people could only know, could only appreciate the magnitude of the price he had paid.

As I hugged his shoes I was suddenly angry! He had done so much, had sacrificed so greatly, and not one of them could possibly understand. No one of those cruel people he and his brothers had labored among knew, or even *cared!* Nor could they, for they were wicked, beyond feeling. Sudden tears streamed down my face as I held tightly to Himni's shoes, and I knew that even if they did not know and appreciate, I did!

And then I picked up his clothing, and suddenly more tears came, unbidden. And, forgive me my lack of faith, at last—at last I truly understood.

There, on the clothing of my youngest son, everywhere it seemed, were repairs. Patches done with fine and tiny stitching, carefully done with great effort that they would not show, stitches that were the loving handiwork not of my son but of a . . . a *Lamanitish* mother, an unknown woman who had mended with her hands and her heart the clothing of *my* child.

Instantly my heart went out to her, a woman whom I would likely never know. I was filled with grief because of the smallness of my spirit, and at last gratitude once again filled my soul—not selfish gratitude for my sons' return, but generous gratitude, I hope, for those who have truly loved them while they were so long away.

And so now as I record this, I understand, and suddenly I see that my loneliness and my sacrifice has been used by God to teach not only me, but at least one other, of love. I see too that my sorrow has been but a type and a shadow of that which God Himself will endure when His Son leaves His presence to come here.

Thus forever will I praise the name of the Lord, my God and my Salvation. In His infinite wisdom and mercy He gave me the loneliness He will one day feel, so that His other children might learn to love my sons as I love them, and His.

From the Book
of Alma we
discover that . . .

The mission to the Lamanites of the four sons of Mosiah is a major ancient American incident. Mormon took his account

of it from Alma's record. Alma seems to have obtained it from
the four brothers themselves, and it comprises nine chapters
of Alma's record.[1]

According to their account, the four brothers, Ammon,
Aaron, Omner, and Himni, feared greatly for their souls because of the wickedness they had perpetrated.[2] In that frame
of mind, and fearing that others too might suffer endless torment as they themselves had come so close to doing,[3] the four
approached their father, King Mosiah, and requested permission to take a few of their friends and go up to the land of
Nephi to declare the word of God to the Lamanites.[4]

Troubled, Mosiah pleaded for many days before the
Lord,[5] and finally obtained the promise that the four would
not only do much good but would be protected as well. At that,
King Mosiah gave his permission.[6]

Taking their unnamed friends, these four brothers departed into the wilderness, embarking upon what was to be a
fourteen-year mission.[7]

Years later King Mosiah waxed old, and, having no heir
that could be reached or that would accept the responsibility,
he gave the sacred records of his people and other items, including the Urim and Thummim, the sword of Laban, and
probably the ball or directors given to Lehi, to Alma the
Younger.[8]

Then, in a unique political move, Mosiah encouraged the
people to have no more kings but to elect judges to rule over
them according to the laws he had established. And because
Mosiah had sought neither riches nor power the people loved
him and did as he suggested, appointing Alma the Younger to
be the first chief judge,[9] Alma having already been ordained
High Priest over the people by his father.[10]

Shortly thereafter Alma the Elder died,[11] as did King
Mosiah.[12]

The fourteen years for both the younger Alma and his
four friends is described thoroughly in the Book of Mormon,[13] though the account of the missionary labors of the sons
of Mosiah deals most with Ammon and to a lesser extent with
Aaron, telling us almost nothing at all about the activities of
Omner and Himni. We know, however, that all four went
from house to house;[14] relied upon the mercies of the people
among whom they labored;[15] taught them in houses, streets,
temples, synagogues, and the wilderness;[16] were cast out,
mocked, spit upon, smote on their cheeks, stoned, bound with

strong cords, and cast into prison. We know too that they were delivered from all this by the power of God.[17]

At the conclusion of their labors, and while they were on their way home to learn the disposition of the people of Zarahemla toward their Lamanite converts,[18] the four missionary brothers and their friends had an unexpected and extremely joyful encounter with Alma the Younger.[19] Alma took the brothers to his own home;[20] the chief judge sent out a letter asking the people what their wishes were concerning the Lamanites;[21] the people agreed to give up the land of Jershon for them[22] and to provide protection for them;[23] and Ammon, with Alma accompanying him, returned with the good news to his converts.[24] While there, Alma told the people of his and his friends' miraculous conversion, and all rejoiced together.[25]

There is no mention in the Book of Mormon whatsoever of the woman who was the mother of these four men, and so the preceding story is completely fictional. She may have been alive upon their return or she may not have been. Whichever, she would, motherlike, have missed them and worried about them a great deal. Additionally, like all mothers of missionaries today, she must have been a remarkably good and faithful woman to allow her sons to go out amidst such dangerous conditions.

Truly did she and her sons, and all who so sacrifice today, choose to live the loftier way.

---

1. Alma 17-26 (see "The Identified" story and "Discovery" note in this volume for more information on Alma and the four sons of Mosiah: Ammon, Aaron, Omner and Himni).
2. Mosiah 28:4.
3. Mosiah 28:2-3.
4. Mosiah 28:1.
5. Mosiah 28:5.
6. Mosiah 28:7.
7. Alma 17:4.
8. Mosiah 28:11-20.
9. Mosiah 29:37-42.
10. Mosiah 29:42.
11. Mosiah 29:45.
12. Mosiah 29:46.
13. Alma 1-16, 17-26.
14. Alma 26:28.
15. Ibid.
16. Alma 26:29.

17. Ibid.
18. Alma 27:15.
19. Alma 27:16.
20. Alma 27:20.
21. Alma 27:21.
22. Alma 27:22.
23. Alma 27:23-24.
24. Alma 27:25.
25. Ibid.

The Identified

At first the old man saw only five, but of course he knew there were more. There always were. That was why the five were yelling and laughing and mocking as they were.

Slowly he made his way down the road toward them, straining his ears to catch what they were shouting, and wondering as he shuffled along what he was going to do once he got to them. He thought too of the meeting he was going to be late for, worried about it briefly, and knew that others could carry on. He knew too that what he was now going to attempt could be even more important. Could be.

Others would indeed handle the meeting, but could he handle this, old and decrepit as he was? He didn't know, but he was surely going to try. That was the least he could do for these youngsters who understood so little about what they were doing.

He thought then of himself, a humorous and usually painful thing for one his age to do, and for a moment he felt the old self-consciousness about his appearance.

He was not a large man, though he had never been considered small. That, however, had more to do with his waistline rather than with his height, for as an adolescent he had grown out rather than up, making his girth more than ample and thus providing a major foe against which he had waged war for the biggest part of his life.

True victory had never been his, but then neither had defeat. He had simply held his own against truly mountainous growth, and for that he was grateful.

On the other hand, he had kept his hair, and though it was indeed thinning, keeping any of it at all was another victory. Of all the male members of his family his head was most abundantly blessed with foliage, and when those beloved male siblings reminded him of his shortness and portliness he countered with personally gathered intelligence regarding their own shiny and sparsely covered domes. In this there was never maliciousness, only good-natured bantering, but the old man thanked his good fortune each time they met that he still had at least one thing left with which to banter.

Now, as he approached the five young people, he thought of his hair. His eyes crinkled and sparkled with his customary good humor, and again he thought briefly of how he must look to them. They were young, full of life and vitality, trim to the point of thinness, and the boys among them had full heads of hair.

"Ah," he muttered half aloud, "an old horse. That's what I look like, too long out to pasture." Again he grinned. "The cliché is indeed true. How sad it is that youth is wasted on the young. And how sad too that wisdom comes only with my sort of appearance."

A moment or so later, when he was much nearer, the old man saw the other boy and girl. They were silently enduring the verbal abuse and coarse laughter being heaped upon them. But the old man, even with his dimming vision, could see the pain in their eyes as they moved slowly away.

Kindness, he thought to himself as he continued forward. *Will it never become spontaneous?*

"Greetings," he said in his customary manner when he had finally, with much huffing and puffing, arrived. "May peace be with you all."

Three of the young people turned, looked at him momentarily, and then with blank looks turned silently away. The other two didn't even look at him.

Somewhat surprised at their rudeness, the old man

hesitated. But then, recalling similar experiences in other times and in other places, he ignored the slight, quietly exerted himself in a way he had learned to do so well, and took unobtrusive control of the situation.

Moving to where he was between the five and the other two, he put his feet down firmly, faced the most vocal among them, and smiled.

"Lovely morning," he said amiably.

The boy to whom he had spoken stared, turned, and looked blankly at the others. Then he turned back, saw the gentle smile once more, and was almost instantly rendered powerless by it.

"Reminds me of a morning I once heard about," the old man continued quickly, not giving the boy a chance to respond. "It's hot here, though, far too hot for an old man like me. Help me to that tree over there, son. The rest of you come along too. I have a story just itching to come out, and there's no better time than a morning like this to set it free."

And then, before the boy could protest, the old man leaned on the lad's arm and became suddenly weak and frail. The youth, as the old man had known he would, showed the others a look of surprised helplessness, rolled his eyes in obvious frustration, and then began moving slowly toward the tree, helping the old man along. The other four, after an instant's hesitation, followed.

The old man, sure now that they were with him, suddenly stopped. "Here," he yelled as he gestured with his free arm at the two who had been pushed aside and left behind. "The two of you, come here, and be quick about it!"

The boy and girl, watching the new development among their persecuters and wondering at it, now looked at each other in surprise.

"Say," a boy growled. "We don't want—"

Again the old man signaled for the two to follow. "Too good a morning to leave folks out," he said amiably to the five who were with him, "no matter *who* they are."

His meaning was not lost on the five, who suddenly

knew that this old man somehow understood and sympathized. An instant truce was mentally called, and when the old man signaled the third time, there was no more murmuring.

Finally, when the boy and girl started slowly forward, the old man once again allowed himself to be helped toward the tree.

"Well," he said quietly when all were relaxed on the ground around him, the two separated a little from the others, and none paying any more attention than they had to. "Where shall I begin?"

"I don't really care," a girl grumbled almost to herself, but intentionally loud enough for him to hear.

"Me neither," another agreed. "I think this is foolish."

"Maybe," the old man replied quietly. "But I have a story to tell, and I think you will want to hear it."

"Well," the boy who had helped him responded, "I just hope it's funny. I'm bored silly with lectures."

The old man smiled slightly, recalling suddenly the way young people seemed to respond to humor, and remembered too a host of experiences where he had learned to bring laughter and smiles. And so, with a silent prayer that the Lord would forgive him a few gentle liberties with experiences that had been very sacred, he began.

"Four men I speak of," he said quietly. "Their names were Ammon, Aaron, Omner, and Himni. You've perhaps heard of them?"

There were blank stares from all seven. "Ahhh," he sighed. "Well, I must go back a little further than I had supposed. But be that as it may, Ammon, Aaron, Omner, and Himni were brothers, not good brothers but brothers still. And they were friends with Alma the Younger."

Recognition suddenly showed on most of the faces, but the old man ignored it and continued, speaking now as rapidly as he could and not pausing at all between sentences.

"Alma the Younger was the son of Alma the Elder,

who was called Alma the Elder not because in the
Church he was Elder Alma, although he was that too be-
cause he was of course the Prophet and all prophets are
called Elder, but because he was older than Alma the
Younger, and that was why he was called Alma the Elder,
and his son, who was younger, was called Alma the
Younger, and that had nothing at all to do with the
Church but with the fact that one was older than the
other, and so he was Alma the Elder and the other was
Alma the Younger."

Some of the young people were smiling now, and
even the ones who weren't were watching him, listening.
The elderly gentleman, delighted that his tongue still
had a little of the old agility, continued.

"So Alma the Younger and Ammon, Aaron, Omner,
and Himni were great friends, and all of them, to a
man, were wicked. They truly were. They were idolatrous, they were liars, they were masters with flattering
words, and they were always surrounded by people who
paid them homage and wanted to be their friends. In
short, they were never lonely.

"Elder Alma who was called Alma the Elder would
travel around the land conducting meetings and declaring the word of the Lord, and when the meetings were
over the people would leave and right outside would be
Alma the Younger and Ammon, Aaron, Omner, and
Himni, all of them lying and speaking out against the
things Alma the Elder had been saying.

"'Don't believe that old fool,' they would say. 'He's
just trying to enslave you and lead you astray. Come follow us. Our style of living is right for our times, and you
will definitely enjoy it.'

"Sadly, many of the righteous believed these five and
were led off into great wickedness and darkness. As for
the others, who would *not* listen, Alma the Younger and
his four friends would mock them and heap abuse upon
them until even the best of them would be so intimidated
and emotionally destroyed that they could no longer be
effective in the Lord's work. They didn't believe in themselves any longer, and I'm sure you know that when a

person doesn't believe in himself, it is almost impossible for him to truly believe in God. Right?"

The seven slowly nodded.

"As you can understand," the old man went on, "this was a great trial for Alma the Elder, for not only were the members of God's church being led astray and destroyed, but it was being done by his own son and four sons of his good friend King Mosiah."

Now the young people looked at each other again. Another name had struck a chord of memory. They had definitely heard of King Mosiah.

"Being the man of faith that he was, Alma the Elder did a lot of praying," the old man continued, "and I imagine that one night in desperation he knelt down and told the Lord that something drastic needed to be done.

"Well, I can't speak for the Lord, at least on this matter, but it seems likely that He too felt things had gone on long enough. So, calling in one of his angels, God told him that he was being sent on a mission. He gave the angel instructions, the angel slipped into a cloud and departed, and Alma the Elder's prayer was about to be answered."

The old man now paused and looked around at the glorious day. "As I said earlier," he went on, "that happened on a morning much as this. The sun was bright in the cloudless sky, the scent of flowers filled the warm air, the lovely calls of birds lent a sweetness to the day, and the five friends, Alma the Younger, Ammon, Aaron, Omner, and Himni, were oblivious to all of it.

"They were walking together down a trail through the forest on their way from one place of spiritual destruction to another, their hearts filled with thoughts of new deviltry and their souls exulting in their wickedness, caring not for the beauties of the world God had made nor for the eternal nature of the numerous souls they were destroying. As I said, they were very evil young men.

"Suddenly, however, their world was turned over and all things began to change. A cloud descended from the cloudless sky, a cloud they couldn't help but notice. It settled onto the path before them, and an angel stepped out, walked up to them, and spoke with a voice so thunderous it caused the ground to shake. All five immediately fell to the earth.

"'I am an angel,' he said by way of introduction, and all five believed him immediately. After all, he had stepped forth from a cloud and then walked up and introduced himself so loudly it had caused an earthquake. With all of that, it was very difficult to doubt him. And believe me, those five friends didn't.

"Many things the angel told those boys after he'd had them stand up again, but I suppose his main message was this: *'If you want to destroy yourselves and be cast off, that's fine. Go ahead. But stop dragging other people down with you! Stop teaching them falsely, and stop destroying their spirits with your wicked mockery and pride. Do you understand?'*

"Well, they most certainly did, so the angel pulled out another earthquake, tossed it into the trail, and watched as Alma the Younger and Ammon, Aaron, Omner, and Himni fell to the earth again. Then he got into his cloud and departed.

"After he had gone the four sons of Mosiah stood up, but young Alma had lost all his strength and had become dumb and couldn't move. Finally the four brothers made a stretcher, loaded Alma on it, and took him home to his father's house. And you know, what happened then is sort of a sad commentary on Alma the Younger's life."

The old man paused and looked from one face to the other, amazed that all were listening so intently. Mentally he thanked the Lord for what had happened so far, asked for strength to continue, and then went on.

"Do you young people know how hard it is to be a parent? Oh of course you don't, for you have yet to become one. But I am a father, and I'll tell you, it isn't easy! Now I've never been a mother, of course, but I've lived with one variety or another all of my life, either as my own or married to the one who mothered my children, and I don't think it's easy for them either. But as I said, I *have* been a father, and I can tell you this, some days that's awful. It is hard, and among other things, it is embarrassing.

"Now I have nine children, and all of them are girls but seven. That may be a part of my problem. But whatever, let me tell you what it's like. I was conducting a meeting one day, when suddenly I noticed all heads turned toward the back. There were lots of grins and snickers and I was wondering what was going on when I saw this little boy way at the back, coming up toward where I was sitting. As I watched I suddenly realized that the child had taken off all his clothes. I smiled too then, thinking of how embarrassed the boy's parents would be when they found out. Then the child got closer and I realized he was my son."

The seven young people all laughed, but the old man paid no attention, continuing. "Of course I went after him, but he ran the other way, and then everybody was grinning and chuckling at *me*. I'll tell you, it is awful what children put their parents through. Still, I like mine. I really do. If one of them was brought home on a stretcher I'd feel awful. I hate to see any of them in pain, and I don't think I'm too different from most other parents. When one hurts I'd gladly take his place. Thank goodness I can't, but I'm sure I would if I could. That's what makes Alma the Elder's reaction so sad.

"You see, when his son was brought in unconscious, his father, who hated just as I do to see his son in pain, *rejoiced*. Why? Because that was the best condition his son had come home in, in years.

"Now that's sad. I hope none of you ever allow Satan to induce you to become so wicked that your parents rejoice when you are carried in on a stretcher. I honestly do.

"Still, Alma the Younger had reached such a point of wickedness. So, because of the faith and prayers of his father and other righteous people, the Lord had struck him down and was now about to convert him the hard way.

"For two days and two nights that young man was unconscious while the Lord was letting his sinful spirit go through the pains of hell. Finally, however, young Alma

stood upon his feet and declared that the Lord had redeemed him and that he was no longer an evil man.

"Now I'd like to tell you more about *that*, but it was
very sacred, and so I'll save it for a time when it's more
appropriate. I will say, however, that young Alma's redemption came through the goodness and mercy of God,
and it was a wondrous thing indeed.

"Alma's four friends, Ammon, Aaron, Omner, and
Himni, also having been touched by the Spirit of the
Lord during the past two days and likewise redeemed,
agreed with his decision and conviction. So together the
five of them set out to reconvert all the people they had
once led astray.

"However, that brings up an interesting truth, one
we all must learn sooner or later: It is a lot easier to lead
people astray than it is to bring them back to the truth. In
trying to do that, Alma the Younger and his friends were
persecuted, beaten and mocked, all their one-time
friends turned against them, and thus they became very
lonely young men. And besides, almost none of their
former friends listened to them. Yet they had chosen the
right way, the loftier way, and despite its difficulties they
stayed with it.

"Some time later Alma the Younger was called to be
the Prophet, and his four friends, Ammon, Aaron,
Omner, and Himni, decided they wanted to go on missions. They submitted their requests, felt thankful as the
Lord calmed the fears of their parents, and were called
on a fourteen-year mission to the Lamanites."

There was a surprised look from two of the girls, and
the old man nodded. "That's right. Fourteen years on
a mission among our most dangerous enemies. How
would you like to wait for your boyfriends for fourteen
years? On the other hand, how would you boys like to
serve a fourteen-year mission where people are all the
time trying to take your life?"

The seven looked at each other silently. Such an idea
seemed almost beyond their comprehension.

"Well," the old man went on, "in spite of such opposition they had wonderful missions. They spent a great deal of time in prisons and fighting with their swords, they learned to love lots of enemies, they spent hours and hours declaring the word of God, and so on. They also had much success, and over the course of time baptized many into the Church.

"Finally their fourteen years were over and they were on their way home. But you know how missionaries are. They wanted those at home to meet their converts. That, and a little trouble with their nonconverted brethren, convinced the righteous Lamanites to go home with the four brothers. So they all lined up with their flocks and herds and children, and soon miles and miles of converts and property were winding up the road toward Zarahemla.

"Along the way they happened to meet Alma the Younger, who had worried for all fourteen years about how his best friends were doing. And I suppose you can imagine the joy with which they greeted each other.

"Of course, once the four brothers and their followers got to Zarahemla, no one had a home big enough to house all the converted Lamanites, so the Nephites gave them a land called Jershon. The converted Lamanites moved in, set up their homes, and all lived righteously. And now I'm ready to begin my story."

There was a gasp from two or three of the youths, and the others laughed. "You mean that wasn't it?" a girl asked, giggling.

The old man shook his head and smiled, looking from her to each of the others and back again. They were together now, all seven. They had moved closer to the old man and were no longer even aware of each other except in a very basic way, and finally there were no outsiders among them. That meant it was time—time to get to the point.

"One morning," he said after taking a deep breath, "just after breakfast, there was a loud knock on the front door of the land of Jershon. Someone opened it, and there stood a fine-looking man, very well dressed and courteous, who was smiling pleasantly.

"'Hello,' he said. 'I'm a preacher. May I come in?'

"The people, who now called themselves the people of Ammon, welcomed him joyfully, for they delighted in nothing so much as hearing the word of God. Hastily dragging out a pulpit they ushered him to it and then took their seats, eagerly awaiting the man's words.

"'I'm here,' he said, 'to declare the truth to you.'

"The people nodded agreeably, for they loved the truth. Sensing that he had already developed a rapport with his audience, the fine-looking man went on.

"'The first truth I will tell you,' he cried, speaking powerfully and with great conviction, 'is that to be happy you must each become concerned with the management of the creature self. That means if you want to get ahead in this world, you must do it by stepping on other people. The fastest way to climb is by dragging others down until they are below you. Be concerned for yourself only. Use your brains and intelligence for *you* and for no one else.

"'Again, it doesn't matter if you hurt others; that is their problem. If they are different, make fun of them. That will elevate you. If they believe the foolish traditions of their fathers, mock them. That will make you their conqueror. I tell you, there is nothing you can do that is evil or bad or a crime, if you do it by your own strength and intelligence.'"

Now the seven were staring uncomfortably at one another. They knew such teachings were false, and they wondered that the old man should repeat them.

"Needless to say," he went on, "the people, just as you, were surprised. What this man was teaching was certainly a different kind of truth from what Ammon and his brothers had taught them. In fact, it was exactly opposite to what they had been taught, and the converted Lamanites told the man so.

"'Perhaps it is,' he declared mockingly, 'but that doesn't change things. I've told you a truth. And now, here is another truth, so pay attention. No matter what you have heard or read, I tell you that there never has been, is not, and *never will be*, a being called Jesus Christ.'

"'Wait a minute,' someone said. 'Are you an anti-Christ?'

"'I certainly am,' the man quickly answered.

"'What's your name?'"

"'Korihor,' the man replied proudly.

"'Oh yes,' the people said, looking uneasily at one another. 'We've heard of you. We have no more desire to hear you.'

"Korihor laughed, and with his great ability he began to mock and ridicule, making the people feel foolish and ignorant and less than they were. But those converted Lamanites were wise, and they said to each other: 'Throw a rope on him, quick, and let us take him to Ammon. He'll know what to do.'

"They did, and soon Ammon was questioning Korihor and recalling his own evil days and testifying to the anti-Christ of things to come. However, Korihor steadfastly maintained that he was declaring truth, and just as steadfastly he refused to repent of his position.

"Ammon then gave him a choice: either repent or leave. Korihor abruptly left.

"Outside, Korihor crossed the street to the land of Gideon and began to declare his same selfish message to those people. But again he was bound up and taken to their leader. He still refused to repent, and so he was finally delivered to Alma the Younger and to the man who was the new chief judge over all the land.

"Alma questioned him, Korihor responded defiantly and with great swelling words, and finally Alma knew that he had no choice but to declare the man's true position and call him to full repentance.

"'Korihor,' he said 'you say you do not believe, but you do. The trouble is that Satan has hold on your heart and you are filled with a lying spirit.'

"'You can't call me a liar,' Korihor cried angrily.

"'I just did,' Alma calmly replied.

"'Well,' Korihor stated, 'I'm not a liar. I speak the truth. And I'll tell you something else. I won't believe unless you show me a sign.'"

The old man paused and looked slowly around at the seven young people, all of whom were listening intently. "Let me tell you," he said, looking at each of them in turn. "That was dumb. Never, never, *never* ask a prophet for a sign. Don't even ask a local leader for one. Such a request just isn't smart.

"But then, neither was Korihor. Somewhere he'd lost a screw. Satan had worked him loose, and he'd finally fallen all the way off the shelf. That's how bad he was.

"Of course, Alma felt terrible about Korihor's demand, for he knew what would happen to the man if he didn't repent. Remember, at one time Alma had felt the chains of hell and the power of God himself, and his heart ached at the thought of what was going to happen to Korihor.

"'You surely don't want a sign,' Alma replied pleadingly.

"Korihor answered firmly, 'Oh yes I do!'

"'No you don't,' Alma implored. 'Please don't.'

"'But yes I do,' Korihor stated arrogantly, his voice as defiant as ever.

"'Well,' Alma finally responded, his heart filled with sadness, 'it is better that your soul should be lost than that you should be the means of destroying many others. If you persist in your foolishness, the Lord will strike you dumb. That will be your sign.'

"'I don't believe there is a Lord,' Korihor declared with a laugh, still bound up in his own foolishness. 'And I won't believe, not unless you show me a sign!'

"'Very well,' Alma replied with resignation. 'Korihor, in the name of God, be thou struck dumb!'"

Again the old man paused and looked around. "Frankly, young people," he said quietly, "that doesn't seem like much of a challenge for either God *or* his prophet, striking Korihor dumb. After all, he was already mostly there anyway."

Everyone chuckled. The old man watched their faces carefully and, when it was time, he went on.

"After Korihor had been smitten by the Lord so that he could have no more utterance, the Chief Judge wrote him a note and asked him if he had changed his mind and now believed. Korihor, who suddenly could make no noise at all, took up the pen and wrote back.

"'Yes,' he wrote. 'I know I am dumb, and I know that

the Lord did it. Besides that, I knew all along that there was a God. However, Satan deceived me, for he came to me like an angel and told me to declare that there was no God. He also told me other things, and told me to declare them as well. I did, even as he commanded, and I was soon at the point where I believed those things myself. Truly they seemed right to me.

"'But now I see the error of my ways, and I am uncomfortable with this curse. Therefore, Alma, because I am converted, take it away and heal me. Quickly, please.'

"'No,' Alma responded after a moment's thought. 'You earned it, Korihor. You'd better keep it for a while.'

"Of course Korihor lost his job," the old man went on slowly. "Satan doesn't employ preachers who can't preach. So he became a beggar, going from house to house begging for food. And one day, over in the land of the Zoramites, as he was crossing a street, some young people in a fancy chariot came speeding around the corner and ran upon him, their horses trodding the abandoned anti-Christ down into the dust of the earth. That, my young friends, was the last of Korihor. In the end he was let down even by the devil, and now he will be known forever as an anti-Christ."

Again the old man paused and looked around at the seven young people, all of whom were intently silent, waiting for his next words.

"Do you suppose you would recognize an anti-Christ if you saw one today?" he asked quietly.

The young people looked at one another. "Yes, we would," they all agreed.

"How?" the old man asked.

"He'd be against Christ," one of them declared quickly. The others nodded in agreement.

"That's right," the old man stated. "He or she would be against Christ. But what does that mean?"

The young people looked at each other blankly. The old man let them think for a minute, and then once again he took up the slack in the silence of the morning.

"Christ's message is a message of love," he said finally. "He loves all of us equally. To believe that is to have a testimony. Christ then asks us, after we have such a testimony, to do two things with it and with the love he gives us. The first is to love ourselves in a respectful way, or to have self-respect. The second is equally important, and it is to love purely, as Christ does, *everyone* who is around us.

"Young people, an anti-Christ would be one who attempted to destroy, in whatever manner, one or both of those things. He would destroy either God-given testimony or he would destroy God-given love and self-esteem. Don't you agree?"

Each of the seven nodded solemnly.

"I thought you would," the old man said gently. "But now let me ask you another question, a more difficult one. Wouldn't self-esteem be destroyed in a person if they are being mocked, or ridiculed, or laughed at, or being made fun of, no matter how poor they might seem, no matter how different they might appear to be, no matter how far they are from being a member of the popular crowd?

"Spoken even more plainly, could five young people, laughing at and making fun of two others, be anything other than anti-Christs?"

There was an uncomfortable silence, and most of the eyes in the group dropped.

"Tell me," the old man asked softly, "who *are* anti-Christs today? *Who are we?*"

In the total silence of self-examination that followed, the old man rose slowly to his feet. "God has given us such a beautiful morning," he said easily as he looked down upon the group. "It is so filled with his love. Should we not keep it that way?"

Stepping lightly, the old man started to move away, his heart giving thanks to God that the young people had listened while his mind moved ahead to other already-delayed responsibilities.

"Uh . . . Sir?" a boy suddenly asked as he rose to his feet behind the old man.

"Yes?" the story-teller responded.

"Uh . . . thank you for . . . for stopping us."

"You're welcome."

"We . . . uh . . . well, just thank you," the boy added quietly.

The old man nodded silently.

"How did you know?" a girl then asked, her quavering voice filled with great shame. "Wh . . . what we were doing, I mean."

The man smiled sadly. "After one has had as much to do with anti-Christs as I have, from both sides of the issue, such people become terribly obvious."

"Both sides?" several echoed in surprise and confusion.

"Yes," the graying but hardly balding old man replied quietly as his eyes veiled over with shame. "Both sides. You see, I have been there. I *know*! I am called Ammon. I am one of the five I have told you of who once fought against Christ. Now I fight in His behalf, and I pray each day that my small efforts to bring His love to others will be enough to show Him my terrible sorrow over past sins."

Then, while the young people stared after him, the old man turned and moved slowly, painfully away.

From the Books
of Mosiah and Alma
we discover that . . .

The preceding story covers a broad span of time, beginning somewhere between 120 and 100 B.C.[1] and ending with Korihor's death at around 74 B.C.[2] As the account began, Alma the Elder was the prophet over the Church and Mosiah was king.[3] The Church was undergoing a great deal of persecution,[4] and so King Mosiah made such activity illegal.[5]

Among the persecutors was Alma the son of Alma, known as Alma the Younger. The scriptures tell us that he was a wicked and idolatrous man and that he was a gifted speaker.[6] Alma the Younger was joined in his activities against the

Church by four of the songs of King Mosiah, whose names were Ammon, Aaron, Omner, and Himni.[7] Despite the laws of the land and of God they continued to persecute the Church and destroy its members.[8]

One day, as they were traveling, an angel appeared to all five of them.[9] The angel descended in a cloud and spoke to them, and when he spoke his voice was as thunder, shaking the earth.[10] All five young men fell to the earth in astonishment,[11] and at first they didn't understand the angel's words.[12] The angel announced to Alma that he had come in response to his father's prayers.[13] He then demanded that they arise,[14] and finally he declared his identity.[15] He apparently spoke mainly to Alma and told him many things, though his main message was that it was Alma's decision whether or not to be cast off, but that whatever he decided, he was to stop destroying others.[16]

When the angel departed, Alma fell to the earth again and became weak and dumb.[17] The four sons of Mosiah then carried Alma to the home of his father,[18] who immediately rejoiced.[19] The senior Alma then called together the priests, and all commenced a fast that Alma's limbs would receive strength and that he would be able to open his mouth and speak—all to the intent that the people could see the glory of God.[20]

For two days and two nights they fasted.[21] Then Alma recovered, stood up, declared his repentance, and bore testimony to the divinity of Jesus Christ and his mission of redemption for all mankind.[22]

From that day forward Alma the Younger and the four sons of Mosiah, who now understood what jeopardy their eternal lives were actually in,[23] worked tirelessly to reclaim the souls of those they had originally led astray.[24] They bore much affliction and persecution, yet they did much good and brought many back to a knowledge of their Redeemer.[25] It was at this point that the sons of Mosiah requested and received permission to go on missions to the Lamanites.[26]

During the absence of his sons, King Mosiah started the reign of the judges (91 B.C.),[27] and Alma the Younger was appointed the first chief judge.[28] He was also High Priest over the Church, having had that office conferred upon him by his father.[29]

Finally, after fourteen years of service in the land of Nephi among the Lamanites,[30] the sons of Mosiah gathered up those who had heeded their message and returned to the land of

Zarahemla.[31] On the way they met their old friend Alma the Younger, and the reunion was indeed joyful.[32]

In Zarahemla, the Lamanites, who had called themselves the Anti-Nephi-Lehies,[33] were given the land of Jershon for their inheritance. It was located on the east by the sea and south of the land Bountiful.[34] There they became known as the people of Ammon.[35]

The records tell us that these people were a great example to the Nephites, for they were perfectly upright and honest, and they were firm in their testimony of the Lord.[36] Alma, thrilled with the goodness of their souls, gave them a prophet's blessing[37] and waxed eloquent about the desire of him and his four friends, which was to bring souls to God.[38]

Apparently it was in Zarahemla that Korihor first made his appearance, taught his doctrines, and began to win converts.[39] There we learn more fully of his beliefs and activities. He declared that there would be no Christ.[40] He also taught that man must get ahead according to the management of his creature needs[41] and that therefore he could do nothing that was wrong or a crime.[42] He also taught that there was no immorality, for, in his view, life ended forever with death, and so it could not matter how immoral a man or woman was.[43]

In Jershon he taught the same things, but the people of Ammon, being wise to wickedness,[44] bound him and took him to Ammon.[45] Ammon deported Korihor, who went into the land of Gideon, taught his philosophy there, and was bound again and taken to their leader.[46] From there, still bound, he was taken back to Zarahemla and brought before Alma the prophet and the man who was the new chief judge.[47]

There, with great swelling words, Korihor defended himself.[48] Alma, who had once been an anti-Christ himself, began to question Korihor in an effort to show him the error of his thinking.[49] When Korihor refused to listen, Alma informed him that he was filled with a lying spirit,[50] and at that, Korihor asked for a sign.[51]

Alma did his best to discourage Korihor's request,[52] but the anti-Christ was adamant.[53] Alma described what the sign would be and again asked Korihor to repent,[54] but Korihor stubbornly refused,[55] and so Alma, by the power of the priesthood and in the name of God, declared that Korihor would be struck dumb. Instantly it was accomplished.[56]

The Chief Judge then wrote Korihor, asking if he believed. (Was he deaf as well? We don't know, but it is possible.

A later clue might bear this supposition out.) Korihor answered in writing, saying that he did, and that he had believed all along. Only, Satan had appeared to him as an angel and had taught him all that he should say. He had obeyed Satan, had enjoyed the flattery and success, and had come to believe his lies himself, thus bringing upon himself his curse.[57] He then pleaded with Alma that the curse be taken away.[58]

Alma, knowing that Korihor would go back to his wickedness if the curse were removed, left the issue up to God. The curse stayed.[59]

Korihor then became a beggar,[60] and one day in the land of the Zoramites he was run upon and trodden down and killed.[61] (Perhaps he couldn't hear the approaching horses—this is the only clue, other than the Chief Judge writing him his question, that might indicate Korihor's possible deafness.)

Korihor's story is concluded by Mormon, who points out succinctly that the devil does not support his children at the last day but speedily drags each of them down to hell.[62]

The preceding story relates a fictional conversation and is fictional in its description of Ammon's physical appearance as well. Nevertheless, there is no doubt that Ammon and his brothers, throughout their lives, felt godly sorrow over their past sins and did all in their power to stop others from making the same painful mistakes they had made. Truly their commitment took them to the loftier way.

---

1. Mosiah 27:1, footnote.
2. Alma 30:31, footnote.
3. Mosiah 27:1.
4. Mosiah 27:1-2.
5. Mosiah 27:2.
6. Mosiah 27:8.
7. Mosiah 27:34.
8. Mosiah 27:8, 10.
9. Mosiah 27:11.
10. Ibid.
11. Mosiah 27:12.
12. Ibid.
13. Mosiah 27:14.
14. Mosiah 27:13.
15. Mosiah 27:14.
16. Mosiah 27:16.
17. Mosiah 27:18-19.
18. Mosiah 27:19.
19. Mosiah 27:20.

20. Mosiah 27:22.
21. Mosiah 27:23.
22. Mosiah 27:24-31.
23. Mosiah 28:4.
24. Mosiah 27:35.
25. Mosiah 27:32-37.
26. Mosiah 28:1 (see "The Mother" story and "Discovery" note in this volume for further information on the mission of the four sons of Mosiah)
27. Mosiah 29:11.
28. Mosiah 29:42.
29. Ibid.
30. Alma 17:4.
31. Alma 27:2-5.
32. Alma 27:16.
33. Alma 23:17.
34. Alma 27:22.
35. Alma 27:26.
36. Alma 27:27.
37. Alma 29:16-17.
38. Alma 29:9.
39. Alma 30:6.
40. Alma 30:12-16.
41. Alma 30:17.
42. Ibid.
43. Alma 30:18.
44. Alma 30:20.
45. Ibid.
46. Alma 30:21.
47. Alma 30:29-30.
48. Alma 30:31.
49. Alma 30:34-41.
50. Alma 30:42.
51. Alma 30:43.
52. Alma 30:44, 46.
53. Alma 30:45.
54. Alma 30:47.
55. Alma 30:48.
56. Alma 30:49-50.
57. Alma 30:52-53.
58. Alma 30:54.
59. Alma 30:55.
60. Alma 30:56.
61. Alma 30:59.
62. Alma 30:60.

The Price

Lightning flashed and thunder rumbled back in the mountains, and the man shrank against one of the many boulders scattered along the top of the wall, doing his best to hide. The wind was strong and rising, and he knew it was going to rain again. Quickly he glanced at the sky, but it was so dark he could see no detail of the clouds, just a solid blackness. However, he did see the reflection of the next flash of lightning on the rain-slick rocks of the wall upon which he lay. He saw it too on the rain-wet leaves and grass below, and he knew he could put it off no longer. It was time to go.

Far-off thunder rumbled once more. The man shivered involuntarily, and he wondered. Actually it was a good night for what he was planning to do. There was too much noise to hear clearly. The low clouds would help muffle any sounds of fighting, and the constant movement of the trees and brush would help hide his movements. Yet still he wondered, shivered again, and thought suddenly of the possibility of dying.

He'd not considered that before, not often anyway, and he'd never felt like this. Maybe his feelings were a sign, a premonition. But what if he did get killed? Would it really make that much difference? Of course, he wanted to live, was desperate to do so, in fact. But should death

45

come would he fear? No, he knew he wouldn't. He was as ready as he'd ever been.

As he thought of it, the only pain he felt when he thought of death, the only hollowness that ached in his abdomen, was for his family, his sweetheart and the little ones who were already so big that he hardly recognized them on the rare occasions when he was home. But as to death itself, that would be a small price to pay if he could only accomplish what he had set out to do, if he could only bring about the good his secret mission might achieve.

Holding his weapon ready he slid down his wet rope. He left the rope in place for his return and then slipped away through the trees. Coming to a steep bank, he eased his way down it by passing himself from tree to tree, and, at the bottom, close against a massive tree trunk, he listened once more.

Nothing. Nothing but the wind and a slight spattering as water fell from the restless leaves above. Stooping at the trickle of a stream that ran beside him, he scooped his fingers into its clear coldness, drank quickly, splashed his face with water, and finally ran his wet fingers through his hair.

War! How he hated it. How he hated the senseless destruction of property, of people, of families, of spirituality. Objectively he looked at himself, recognizing that war had affected and perhaps destroyed him as well. He knew he had become hardened, and he wondered if he would ever again be the man of gentleness his wife had married. Now he was simply a machine, a mechanism for destruction, a man who somehow still loved his fellow-men but who suddenly found himself on a self-imposed mission where he hoped to bring death to another. And at that he wondered, he truly did.

He started to move out from behind the tree, then stopped abruptly. There was a faint sound of something moving down in the canyon. He listened . . . The wind had slowed, and in the sodden silence a tiny sound came to his ears. Barely audible. Something . . . someone was moving down below.

Breathless he held himself, aware that somebody or something could hear also, and may already have heard him. Should he go back? Should he climb back to the wall and wait for another night, another time when things might work out a little better? After all, there were—

But no! He could not go back! He could not allow the life of this murderer, this . . . this anti-Christ, to go on. The man was beyond the reach of the law, beyond the reach of justice, and there was no other way. Somehow he must find him and put an end to his wanton disregard for the lives and rights of others, just as he had put an end to the life of the man's evil brother some five years before. Then he had had the thought his action would end the conflict, but now he could see that the younger brother, Ammoron, was even more evil and power-hungry than the older Amalickiah had been. Nor would it ever end until both had been laid low in the dust and the people they led rendered leaderless. No, he had to go on—he had to do it. This senseless conflict would never end unless he did.

He crouched, squatting at the foot of the tree, and then he moved suddenly, swiftly, staying low. For an instant he was in the open, but then his body merged with the darkness of a clump of brush, and again he was hidden, invisible.

Lightning flashed and thunder growled, closer this time, and the man held still, waiting, listening. Someone was there, he was certain of it. Yet he had known there would be. Ammoron was crafty, careful, suspicious; more, in fact, than any true Lamanite would have been. Yet it was always so with Nephites who had departed from the truth. In all ways they were more evil than the ones they joined.

Himself being a murderer, Ammoron would suspect all others of the same fault, and so he would be taking no chances. Thus there would be guards, at least one, perhaps several, and the man would simply have to find a way to get past them.

He strained his ears for sound but heard nothing. He straightened up, keeping himself merged with the brush, and then moved away. He was good at this, and he knew it. But was he as good as the man who was out there? Was he even half as good?

He saw the shine of water from the river far below and mentally calculated the distance to it. Ammoron's abode was near the river, or so he had been told. But could he get there without being seen? The brush on his right, between himself and the water, seemed to be an impenetrable wall. He crouched again, trying to identify the shapes around him.

Did something move? Had he heard something, or was it his imagination? Slowly he eased his only weapon forward, and in doing so he accidentally brushed the limbs of some willow.

Instantly there was a soft twang and a swish; he froze, not even looking to the side. If he moved now, he would be dead. The guard, if that was what he was, had fired at what he believed was him, and waited now for movement. The slightest motion, the slightest sound, and another arrow would be loosed, more accurate this time. So the man held still, drawing slow, careful breaths, waiting.

The night was suddenly very still. Along the tiny stream were a number of towering trees, then smaller ones and a great deal of brush. Near the ground were frequent gaps, and if a man could get low enough, and find them—

Suddenly a small bird burst forth from the brush before him. Another arrow whirred past, and then the man heard an almost silent chuckle as the guard realized his mistake and pulled back.

Crouching, the man took advantage of the momentary lapse in the guard's attention, and he quickly worked his way forward, keeping close to the wet earth, pausing frequently to listen for movement. The wind that had quieted for a time was now beginning to rise again, but it had shifted around and was coming from the storm. The lightning also was nearer, the rumble of thunder was louder, and he knew it would be only moments until there was rain, perhaps a great deal of it. If only—

The crash of thunder, when it suddenly came, was deafening and was nearly simultaneous with the brilliant stab of lightning. In the brief glare they saw each other, he and the Lamanite guard, but the Lamanite was luckier, for he was turned sideways. The man threw himself forward, hitting on his shoulder and rolling, hoping for more brush before the next stab of light. But the lightning came again, too soon, and across the clearing the brush moved. He broke a lifelong habit then and threw his weapon, a javelin, at something he could not clearly see. And in that instant the Lamanite stepped into view a dozen feet away and the man felt sudden pain as an arrow pierced his side. Dropping to the ground he grabbed hold of the shaft, clenched his teeth, and pulled the arrow out. Then he rolled, trying only to get away.

He was hurt, badly so, and now he was unarmed. But still, he had made the Lord a promise, and he knew of no other way to end the terrible bloodshed. After all, hadn't the Lord himself once said that it was better for one man to perish than for an entire nation to dwindle and perish in unbelief? And this man, this Ammoron, had brought about so much death, so much senseless and evil destruction, so much unbelief—

Another arrow hissed through the air above him, and then another. Searching shots. He'd known few who could haft an arrow and loose it so quickly, and he was surprised. Could there be more than one? But no, he'd seen only one man, heard no more than that. There was just one Lamanite guard, one man who was very good at killing. And somehow he had to get past him.

Rolling again he dropped suddenly into a small hollow filled with wet leaves. There he took several deep breaths, pressed a compress of mud and leaves against his wound, dragged himself slowly to his feet, and lunged back in the direction from which the arrows had come. He was hit hard, and in no shape for a fight. Yet if not now, when? And if not him—

Lightning flashed again, vividly, and suddenly the Lamanite was there before him, waiting. But what the guard saw he had not expected, and in surprise he let out a hoarse shout, stepping backward. Quickly the man reached out, lunged forward, fell short, and in that moment felt another arrow sink into his shoulder. Gasping with new pain he scrambled to his feet, lifting with him a stick that his hand had somehow located.

Standing then he swung it. The Lamanite lifted his arm involuntarily to ward off the blow. The stick broke and the man dropped it and dived at his enemy's legs.

The Lamanite tried to step back, tripped accidentally, and went down. He was up again instantly, but the wounded man swung at his face, his fist smashing into the Lamanite's nose. There was a grunt of pain, but there was no quit in him, not in either of them. The man was punching, striking hard, and meanwhile the Lamanite was doing his best to bring another arrow to bear.

But there was little space, and no room to loose an arrow. The bodies of the two men were close together, and no matter how the Lamanite twisted, his opponent held him tight. Then the wounded man struck down with his hand, smashing his fist against the Lamanite's wrist and causing the Lamanite to lose his grip on the bow.

Both men then lunged for it. Slipping on the wet earth, they collided and fell, and then both came up fighting, wildly, desperately. Suddenly the Lamanite slipped and went down again. He tried to roll aside, but the wounded man kicked him in the belly. There was another grunt, and for an instant the Nephite thought it might all be over. But then the Lamanite was on his feet again, leaping upward like a great cat, and viciously he came at the man, clawing at his eyes.

The Nephite staggered back, almost tripping over a stone, and in the light from a sudden flash of lightning the Lamanite stopped, swept up his dropped bow, and was gone into the shadows and the darkness.

Breathing heavily the wounded man dragged himself into the brush, where he lay on his back, gasping.

The arrow in his shoulder would not come out, so he snapped it off and packed mud around it as well as against the wound in his side. Then he rolled onto this hands and knees and began to crawl.

Lightning flashed and thunder rumbled, and he crawled on because there was nothing else to do. His body ached, and his head was a huge hollow drum in which something pounded with terrible pain. His mouth was full of cotton and he could not feel his tongue, but still he pushed onward, still he crawled.

His hands grew bloody. The flesh on them was raw, and the blood seeped into the wet earth behind him, yet he kept on. He had no choice, none at all. It was a high price he was paying, but it was not too high for the good it would do. If he and his family could know peace, if his friends and his loved ones could live without fear and without war, then whatever he was going through would most certainly be worthwhile. He knew that, understood it completely, and the understanding kept him going even when pain flailed at his consciousness and reason told him he could not continue. Only—

Thunk.

Suddenly there was an arrow quivering in the trunk of a tree directly before him. The man focused his eyes and looked at it, not understanding, and in the next flash of lightning another one buried itself in the earth directly beneath his body.

The Lamanite!

Again there was a brief flash of lightning, and in its harsh glare the man saw his enemy crouched off to the side notching another arrow.

The guard had followed him! He had moved around until he was in position, and now he was certain of his kill. The Lamanite was certain of where the wounded man was going, and he was there, ahead, waiting for the next flash of light, waiting—

Turning, the Nephite lunged to his feet and plowed upward, knowing as he did so that he would be expected to go downhill, for that was the way of all wounded things. And, too, it was also where the dark-skinned guard was waiting, his arrow ready to put an end to the man's vital mission.

Falling, he rose and dragged himself forward, fighting the dizziness and the pain, fighting too the steep hillside, wanting only to get away so that he could get to Ammoron before daylight and further death and destruction.

A ghost of a trail opened through the brush before him, and the wounded man lunged up it, coming suddenly to the great wall of the city. Frantically he climbed, digging his fingers into the tight seams between the rocks and dragging himself upward, ignoring the pain and forcing from his mind the thought that he might not make it. With all his heart he wished for his rope, and as he dragged himself up the sheer face of the wall he remembered the lightning and felt fear crawling up and down his spine. The enemy was below, his bow ready and bent, and he waited only for a flash of light—

In desperation the man pulled himself higher, fearing the lightning and knowing that his only hope was to get across the wall unseen and in darkness. Then he could come back lower down and closer to the river, and there might be a chance, a hope—

Then he was on top, lightning suddenly did flash, and in its light he saw one of the boulders left there by those who intended to use them for the defense of the city. It was larger than he was, poised on the edge of the wall, and it seemed ready, waiting. In the light he also saw the Lamanite guard, at the edge of the brush below, raising his bow, and the man knew what he had to do.

Quickly he stepped to the boulder, and in the darkness he tried its weight with his hands. Below there was a twang. A split second later something shattered against the rock near his head, and he knew there was little time. Another flash of lightning, another arrow, and he would never get to Ammoron. He simply could not take another such wound.

Stooping, he grasped the stone, closed his eyes, and paused to gather strength. Then he heaved upward. The rock tipped, grated, then hung. The rain was falling again, and he was soaked with blood and rain. His feet gripping the wall, he strained . . . The boulder tipped, grated, leaned further out, and again there was a shattering against the rock near his head.

Had he moved so that he was now vulnerable? Had the Lamanite shifted position so that—

Alone on the wall the wounded man stood, his body straining beyond its limit, veins swelling in his brow and throbbing in his throat. His muscles were knotted, his eyes were screwed tightly closed, his mouth was drawn open in a grimace that came from the intensity of the pain he was feeling. Only the rock, the boulder—

Suddenly there was a stabbing pain in his side. He gave a last valiant effort and collapsed, and finally the great rock rolled free.

He went to his knees gasping, his mouth wide with pain and the need for air, feeling, as he knelt, the blood coursing down his side, feeling too the rain and sweat dripping from his brow.

With a rattle of gravel the boulder dropped off into the blackness below, silently, surely. Seconds later there was an agonized cry of fear, the sound of wild scrambling, a heavy thrashing, and then an animal-like scream that ended as suddenly as it had begun. Finally there was a splintering crash, a brief chatter of small stones, and then nothing.

Alone then, and knowing he truly was, the man took several deep breaths, filled his mind with a prayer of gratitude, and carefully lowered himself from the wall. Once on the ground he packed more mud and leaves against his shoulder and side, and then he made his way slowly and painfully down the hill toward the river and the dwelling of Ammoron.

Later, hours perhaps, he stood alone outside the dimly lit building where slept Ammoron, the white leader of the Lamanites. In the distance, light from a guard's fire flickered on the under branches of the surrounding trees and was reflected from the smooth face of the dwelling, and the man stood very still, his chest heaving, his hand pressed against the wound in his side, watching.

A night-bird called, and far off a wild animal cried its immeasurable woe to the storm-filled sky. The man listened and watched, but he saw no movement at the fire, so he made his way carefully toward it and was surprised to find the guard asleep. Picking up the man's javelin, he thought of killing him, and suddenly his mind was filled with revulsion that he would even consider such a thing. No, the guard would live, and perhaps one day would learn of this and would thank him.

The man was dizzy as he entered the building, his body reeling with weakness because of his great loss of blood. His head was pounding even harder, his side ached relentlessly, and his shoulder, too, was throbbing. Silently he prayed, pleading with God that he might have the strength to go on, promising anything, even his life now, if he could only put an end to the evil Ammoron and to the great destruction the man had brought about.

Twice he staggered into the wall, but each time he managed to keep his feet and to push ahead, moving as quietly as he could, searching—

And then he was in the sleeping chamber, and in the flickering light from one small oil lamp he saw Ammoron before him, tossing fitfully on his bed.

Slowly the man straightened himself to full height and looked around to make certain that he was alone with this deceitful murderer and leader of the Lamanites. Satisfied that he was, he lifted the javelin he had taken from the guard, braced himself, took a deep breath to slow his dizziness and steady his aim, and threw.

The scream, when it came, was short, for Ammoron died almost instantly, the javelin having pierced his heart. But his scream—his scream—

The twice-wounded Nephite turned to flee but had taken only a few staggering steps back down the hallway when the shape of a man loomed before him. In surprise he recognized the very guard whose life he had spared only moments before. And in the guard's upraised hand flashed the blade of a great battle-sword. Oh, no! Now the guard would never—

Turning, he tried to dodge, but his strength was gone, and with it his agility. Suddenly he felt the fiery smash of the guard's blade, driving him to his knees, and as he tried to pull away another struck into him, from behind.

He fell then against the wall, his pain so great he almost couldn't feel it, and as more guards rushed forward with their weapons ready he looked up, smiled weakly, wiped the blood from where it was suddenly frothing from his mouth, took a deep breath, and spoke.

"He . . . he is gone," he gasped. "I, Teancum, have s—slain the evil Ammoron as I slew his wic—wicked brother Amalickiah. M—may God grant that the price of my life is sufficient that our two peoples, and our children after us, may . . . live . . . in peace."

And, with that, Teancum paid.

From the Book of Alma we discover that . . .

From Nephi and his brothers onward, the Book of Mormon is replete with Nephite-Lamanite conflicts. The particular war upon which the preceding story is based began with pride in the Church, when a group of members wouldn't give heed to the words of Helaman, the son of Alma the Younger.[1] The leader of this group was a man named Amalickiah, whose great desire in life was to be king.[2] His followers were men and women who also desired power, and who had been led by Amalickiah to believe they could get it through him.[3]

These people rebelled;[4] General Moroni rallied the people with his torn coat, which he called the Title of Liberty;[5] Amalickiah saw that he was outnumbered, and so he took those who would go and departed, after a battle with Moroni wherein he lost most of his people,[6] into the Land of Nephi. There he lived with the Lamanites.[7]

What follows in the ancient record is a tale of almost unbelievable treachery and deceit. Amalickiah developed good graces with the Lamanites; stirred up some of them, including the king, to anger against the Nephites; led the Lamanite armies against all Lamanites who wouldn't fight the Nephites; surrendered his armies in a secret agreement with the peacefully inclined Lamanite leader Lehonti; poisoned Lehonti that he died; took over *all* the Lamanite armies; upon his return had his servants slay the king; told the king's wife her servants had done it; and married the queen. So, he obtained in every way possible the Lamanite kingdom, becoming in the process even more wicked and ferocious than they.[8]

In about 72 B.C. Amalickiah led the Lamanites against the Nephites. But Moroni, knowing from inspiration what would come, had prepared well, and Amalickiah was repulsed again and again.[9] Finally in his anger he cursed God and swore to drink the blood of Moroni.[10]

For a time, while Amalickiah prepared the Lamanites for further battle, there was peace. But in the midst of this peace some of the Nephites under a man named Morianton began to claim the land used by the people of the city of Lehi, also Nephites. This dispute grew sore, but the people of the city of Lehi were in the right.[11] Moroni prepared to send an army, and so Morianton convinced his people to flee northward.[12] This plan was discovered when Morianton beat a servant girl who fled to Moroni with the information.[13]

Moroni then sent an army after Morianton and his followers, which headed them off before they could escape and thus ensured the solidarity of the Nephites. This army was lead by Teancum, which is the first we hear of him in the Book of Mormon. In the battle that followed, Teancum slew Morianton and stopped the division of the people.[14]

Shortly thereafter Amalickiah again led his Lamanites in an attack, and over a period of time he destroyed many people and took many cities captive.[15] Finally, however, his progress was stopped by Teancum and his armies, who, according to the record, were all mighty soldiers.[16]

Teancum, tired of Amalickiah's wickedness and supposing that his death would bring an end to the bloodshed, took one of his men and stole by night into the camp of Amalickiah. There he drove a javelin through the heart of the wicked king,[17] escaped, and in the morning led his armies as they drove all of the Lamanite army into retreat.[18]

Now Ammoron, Amalackiah's brother, was made king of the Lamanites,[19] and contrary to Teancum's hopes, the war continued, back and forth, for the next three years. In one way or another, Teancum always played a leading role on the side of the Nephites. He led small armies as decoys to draw the Lamanites out,[20] took charge of prisoners of war,[21] fought frequently side by side with Moroni,[22] and all the while chafed under the rule of Ammoron, who he felt was the cause of all the famine and bloodshed and trouble.[23]

Finally Teancum's indignation at the horrors of war waxed so strong that he set out again at night, this time alone, and with a rope scaled the wall of the city where Ammoron was sleeping.[24] Once inside he located Ammoron, cast his javelin, and slew the Lamanite leader.

However, Ammoron cried out before he died, and his cry alerted his guards, who captured Teancum and slew him.[25] Thus died a man who had fought valiantly for his country, a man who Mormon tells us was a true friend of liberty.[26]

Nowhere in the record are there details of Teancum's venture into the city or of his fight prior to his death. Thus the story "The Price" is entirely fictitious except for the above historical notes. We do know, however, that the news of Teancum's death saddened Moroni, who led his armies against the leaderless Lamanites the next day, defeated them, and finally established peace once more in the land.[27]

Teancum, choosing the loftiest and loneliest of ways, had truly brought to pass with his death the peace he so desperately craved during his life.

---

 1. Alma 45:23-24.
 2. Alma 46:1-4.
 3. Ibid.
 4. Alma 46:7.
 5. Alma 46:11-13.
 6. Alma 46:33.
 7. Alma 46:29, 33.
 8. Alma 47:1-36.
 9. Alma 49:25.
10. Alma 49:27.
11. Alma 50:27.
12. Alma 50:29.
13. Alma 50:29-31.

14. Alma 50:35-36.
15. Alma 51:23-27.
16. Alma 51:29-31.
17. Alma 51:32-34.
18. Alma 51:35-37; 52:1-2.
19. Alma 52:3.
20. Alma 52:21-26.
21. Alma 53:3-5.
22. Alma 62:32-34.
23. Alma 62:35.
24. Alma 62:36.
25. Ibid.
26. Alma 62:37.
27. Alma 62:38-42.

The Testimony

Leah stood alone in the dark shade of the trees, her face buried in her hands and her slim body shaking with the great wracking sobs that she could not drive away.

"No!" she whispered. "No . . . it can't be! They couldn't!"

Again she felt her heart racing with fear, and as the sobs came again her mind cried out against the injustice of the thing, the enormous cruelty of it all. It wasn't right . . . it just couldn't be so. Just because she was a Believer, just because her father was so prominent and so . . . so vocal, shouldn't mean that they could all be put to death, that they would all . . . die.

Yet according to her friends they would, if . . . if—

Again Leah's sobs came, and as she fought to control them, her mind rehearsed the events of the past hour. It had been late afternoon, and she and her friends had started home together after lessons. But shortly things had been said, cruel and terrifying things, and she had felt suddenly alone, out of place, unwanted. She had hesitated in her stride, one had noticed, the laughter had commenced, and suddenly she had been truly alone.

"Look at her," one had sneered derisively. "Thinks she's so wonderful and righteous!"

"They all do," another had declared haughtily. "I hate them!"

59

There had been a chorus of agreement. Leah had taken another step backward, and then a different girl spoke, an older girl of perhaps sixteen whose name was Liz. Her voice, filled with knowledge and authority far beyond her age, had created a sudden stillness.

"You can't deny it, either," she had snarled. "I've seen your father, everywhere practically, and I've even seen you with him!"

"I . . ." the girl had stammered. "I wasn't . . . I mean . . . he . . ."

"See?" Liz had stated triumphantly. "I told you she was one of them!"

Suffering under the unaccustomed accusations, Leah's eyes had darted from side to side, had seen nothing but hostility in the faces of the others who had so recently been her friends, and suddenly she had felt great fear rising within her heart. Why, even Ruth had turned against her, Ruth who had been her best friend as long as she could remember.

"Ruth," she had pleaded, holding out her hands, "not you. You can't do this after what we've seen, after what we've felt. You don't know what you're doing."

Ruth had laughed caustically. "I certainly do, and if you were smart you'd deny everything too, before it's too late."

The other girls had giggled, but Leah had ignored them, her eyes never leaving those of her friend. "But Ruth," she had implored, "what about the Spirit? What about all the things we've felt together? I've heard you bear your testimony, and I know that you know."

"Know? Listen, all I know is that I was wrong, and so are you!"

"I'll say," Liz had agreed. "You've been hypnotized, all of you. I know, because I've heard lots of people talk about it. *Everybody* says it's so. Your father's behind it, too, he and all the others who go around trying to make converts. And as far as I'm concerned, you *all* deserve what you're going to get!"

Leah had been stunned. "Liz," she had protested, her voice little more than a pleading whisper, "I thought we were friends. I thought Ruth and I were friends. I thought . . . I thought *all* of us were friends. To turn against me, against us, is . . . is *evil.*"

"Friends with Believers?" Liz had exclaimed, shivering with mock disgust. "What a joke! And who's evil? Us? No! You are, you and the rest of them. You want to enslave us. That's what everybody says, and I believe them. As far as I'm concerned, you'll only be getting what you all deserve. Now the rest of you, come on. Let's get out of here before she contaminates us."

The girls, their faces filled with hostility, had turned and started to move away, and Leah had felt as though her insides were being torn apart. Those girls, they *had* been her friends! Ruth was . . . well, she had been her *best* friend. They had done so much together, had shared so many things, but now—

"Ruth," she had cried. "Don't! Don't listen to them! It will happen, I *know* it will. My father says so. He . . . he . . ."

But it had been no use. No one, not even Ruth, had listened. Suddenly filled with fear, Leah had turned and fled blindly, stopping at last only when she was well hidden beneath the huge trees that grew behind the temple. Then the tears had really come, the tears and the questions. Ruth, oh poor Ruth! What had happened to her and her family, and how had it happened so quickly? For that matter what had happened to her? And . . . and . . .

But what if they were right? Leah had never dared ask herself that question before, had not even dared to think it. But now, when things were happening so fast and the end was getting so close, how could she help it? What if tomorrow came and nothing had changed? What would she do? Where could she hide? What would her father do, her father and mother and all the little ones? And what about all the others, all the other Believers? Would they deny as Ruth and her family had done, or would they stand up and allow themselves to be . . . to be *executed.*

Leah shuddered as she thought of the word. She hated it, hated the thought of dying. She didn't want to

die, could not bear the thought of not living, of not growing up and having her own family, her own husband who
loved her as her father loved her mother. But she would,
tomorrow, and she could do nothing about it, nothing at
all!

Her father had told the family to have faith and to
pray without ceasing, and she had, she had! Only, what
good had it done? For weeks they had all done as her
father had told them to do, all of the Believers uniting,
and still—nothing! Not one single thing to give them
hope, to tell them that their faith was not in vain.

For long moments she looked up at the temple,
bright in the afternoon sun, and she wondered again
how she could possibly know if all the things she had
been taught were true. Many said they were, but many
others said they were false, and she was suddenly so con-
fused that she doubted if she would *ever* know.

Later she paused outside her home, wondering what
she should do. Maybe she could talk to her father. He
somehow made things seem not so bad, and his sense of
humor was so droll that he could almost always make her
laugh. Yet what if Liz and the others were right? What if
all along he had been hypnotizing her, forcing her to
think and believe as he did without her even being aware
that he was doing it? Was it possible?

No, of course it wasn't! He wouldn't, *couldn't* do that.
Besides, some of the things that had happened to her,
some of the special feelings she had felt, had occurred
when her father had been nowhere around.

Of course, Liz and Ruth felt that he had just planted
suggestions in her mind, and she supposed that was possible. But no! He wouldn't do that! He loved her and
would never force her to do or think anything.

But on the other hand, what if he wanted so badly for
her to feel as he did that he had decided to make certain?
That was like fanaticism, and she knew her father was
not a fanatic. Yet lots of people called him that, and how
could a person tell? What if he really was? What *was* a
fanatic? How—

With a sigh of frustration Leah dried her eyes and turned into her home, her mind filled with questions, her heart smothered with fear, and her soul aching for answers she was certain she would never live to hear.

The house was strangely quiet, and Leah found herself walking softly as she moved toward her sleeping corner. Behind the robe that hung there, however, she found her family, or at least most of them. Her mother and all the children but she and Cor were there, kneeling together while her mother softly prayed.

Leah dropped the robe and moved quietly back, waiting, trying not to listen to her mother's prayer but listening anyway, and feeling strangely touched as she heard her mother pleading that Leah and the other children would have the strength and courage to resist evil.

Oh, how could her mother be so certain that she was being listened to? And how did she know what was evil? How could her mother or her father or anyone else, for that matter, tell?

Leah then wondered where her father was. He was usually home at this time of day, and—

What if he had already been taken by the . . . the Unbelievers? The thought, sudden as it was, left her with such a hollow pain that new tears instantly filled her eyes, and she realized, just as suddenly, how much she loved him.

"Dear Heavenly Father," she found herself praying as the tears fled silently down her cheeks, "please protect my father, and . . . and . . . Oh dear God, I don't want to die!"

And once again Leah covered her face with her hands and began to sob.

Short moments later, Leah felt her mother's hand rest gently on her shoulder. Drying her eyes, she looked up, saw that her mother's face was also tear-streaked, and knew then that her worst fears were horrifyingly true. There was no hope, no respite from the awful fate the Unbelievers had planned for them. Her friends had been right, and at dawn tomorrow—

Suddenly from outside came shouts and laughter, and as Leah and her mother ran to the door, they saw a group of men and women gathering in the street.

"Yea, verily," someone shouted in a cruelly mocking tone, "there stand the chosen of the Lord!"

"Truly," another agreed, "and with morning light they will surely meet him face to face, just as they have been predicting."

A round of laughter greeted the crude humor, and Leah felt her mother standing tall beside her. Looking over, she saw that the woman's face was firm, set with a mixture of anger and fear and pity, and once again Leah wondered.

"Where's the great prophet?" someone called derisively. "Out bringing some of us poor sinners to repentance?"

There was more laughter, but it was stilled momentarily as Leah's mother stepped into the yard. "Oh, that you *would* repent," she cried defiantly. "Oh, that you would, for only then would you learn happiness. Perhaps you might even feel a little kindness, which would surely be a change for all of you."

"Yes," a woman challenged shrilly while Leah stared with surprise at her mother who was so confidently facing these people. "Just as you will know kindness and happiness come morning, when you learn that we will *not* be your slaves. No thank you, O fool. We are happy enough without hearing of your evil nonsense."

Leah's mother shook her head. "No, that is not true. You are not happy, none of you. Happiness is not found in wickedness, in which you choose to grovel, for that is contrary to the ways of eternity. Such were the words of the dark-skinned prophet."

There was another howl of laughter, from all of them this time, and then the man who seemed to be the leader spoke. "Woman, that dark-skinned heathen was a bigger fool than you, and his words were filled with more nonsense. But no matter. He set the date and fixed the time. You have foolishly chosen to believe and follow, and tomorrow you will learn all there is to know about such things as repentance and happiness.

"Remember, woman. First light. Be sure to have your children ready, for we want no nits growing into lice. And don't forget to bring your husband along. He shall have a front-row seat. Why, he'll hear some prophesying tomorrow and see some repenting that he'll remember all the rest of his very short life."

There was more laughter, and gradually the crowd moved away, leaving Leah and her mother alone in the yard.

"Mother," Leah asked pleadingly as they turned toward the house and the wide-eyed younger children, "what are we to do?"

"Do?" the woman replied as she smoothed back her hair and stooped to pick up her baby. "Why, we do as we have been commanded, I suppose. We exercise our faith and trust in the Lord."

"But . . . but what if they kill us?"

"Then, my child, we die. Can that be so bad, though, when we know that we will shortly be with our God and his Son?"

Angrily then Leah turned on her mother, her voice filled with sudden defiance. "That's very easy for you to say, but I don't know that! I don't know where I'll be, and I don't want to die so I can find out! I'm *afraid!*"

Gently the woman put her free arm around her eldest daughter and drew her close. "Neither do any of us want to die," she responded quietly. "I, too, am afraid, dear Leah. I shrink from death with all my heart, and even more I fear your father's; his, yours, and your brothers' and sisters'. Oh, what if I must witness such a scene as that? How can I stand such a thing? It is unthinkable, and my weary heart recoils from such a thought."

"But mother—"

"I know, my Leah. I know what you are saying. And it is true. We could stop it with just one word of denial. Your father and I have spent many days discussing that

very thing. But you and I both know we cannot do that.
Not after seeing and feeling and learning all that we have
seen and felt and learned. As much as we fear death, as
much as we shrink from facing the cruelty the Unbelievers have planned for us, as much as we fear the suffering
of you, our dear children, we shrink even more from the
fear of losing our place with the Lord. Do you understand?"

Leah shook her head. "Mother, it isn't I that needs to
understand. It is you, you and father. Don't you see? *I
don't know!* For myself, I have seen *nothing.* Nothing! *I do
not have a testimony!*"

Leah's mother pulled back, her face filled with surprise and new pain. "But Leah—"

"Mother, I mean it. You speak of angels and signs,
but I have never seen any. Maybe you've noticed that I
don't often pray anymore. And I don't bear testimony
anymore either. Haven't either of you wondered why?"

"I have noticed, but I thought—"

"Yes, I have felt some things that you say came from
the Spirit," Leah continued quickly, "and, yes, I have
heard you and father and some of the others bear testimony, but I don't even *remember* the dark-skinned
prophet you spoke of! I don't know if what you tell me is
true or not. I don't even know whether by denying I
would lose my place with God."

"Oh, my child," Leah's mother whispered, "do not
say such things. You do know! You must!"

"Mother, you still don't understand! I have no
friends left. Not one! Not even Ruth. All of them have
turned against me, and they . . . they *laugh* at me! I can't
stand it when they do that. They tell me that father has
hypnotized me, and I don't know how to answer them.
For all I know, maybe he has. How do you tell? I can't
help it if I doubt. The others call me a fool, and I don't
blame them. I feel like a fool. I also feel lonely, so lonely
and so *afraid!*"

For a long moment Leah's mother looked at her
nearly grown daughter. Then, gently, she placed her

baby down and took her daughter into her arms. They were standing thus when the door crashed open.

Startled, both women jumped and then spun toward the door, fear and anxiety on their faces. But it was only Cor, Leah's ten-year-old brother.

"Mother," he shouted through gasping breath, "those big boys chased me again! They hit me with rocks, and . . . and one of them said I was going to die."

Cor stopped for a breath, and Leah and her mother glanced quickly at each other. "Where's father?" the boy continued. "I've got to tell him. People are shouting awful things about him and us and all the other Believers, and we need to stop them. Father'll get them, you watch! He'll call down fire or something! They can't say things like—"

"Corianton," Leah's mother said, interrupting him. "Settle down for a minute."

"But mother—"

"Listen to me. Leah and I were just going to find your father. We can do that much more quickly if you will watch the little ones for us. And don't be afraid. We'll be back soon."

Cor looked up, a grin spreading across his face. "You bet I'll watch them. And don't worry. I'm not afraid. They can even *kill* me and I won't be afraid. They don't know anything, and I do! I know He's coming."

"Yes, Cor," Leah's mother responded quietly. "He is. Now keep the little ones in the house, and we'll be back as quickly as possible."

Leah's mother smiled and tousled her son's hair. Then she turned once more to Leah. "Come," she said quietly. "We had better hurry."

A little later, as the two moved quietly through the lush foliage that bordered the city, Leah spoke.

"Cor is so naive," she said.

"Not naive, Leah. Filled with faith."

Leah looked quickly at her mother. "That's not faith. He's too young to even know what faith is."

"You knew what it was when you were his age."

"Mother—"

"Leah, you did. All children have pure faith. We are born with it. Then, as we grow, we partake of the things of the world, and we gradually lose it until we actually begin to doubt the very things we have most known were true."

For a moment Leah was silent, thinking. "Well," she finally responded, "maybe that is so and maybe it isn't. But whatever, I do know that it is gone from me. I don't have a testimony anymore at all."

"Are you certain?" Leah's mother asked gently.

"Of course! Why else would I be feeling like I am?"

"Oh, there could be many reasons. But let me ask you a question, and you answer me as honestly as you can. Do you believe in God? Is there a supreme being who knows of you?"

"I . . . I feel that there is, but then I find myself doubting. My mind comes up with all sorts of conflicting ideas, and . . . and I don't know."

"Those are two answers, Leah. What is the one you want to give me most? And while you're answering, remember that the Holy Ghost deals more with our feelings and emotions than with any other part of us."

"Then I suppose," Leah answered slowly, "that I believe. At least I think maybe I believe in God."

"When you pray, describe whom you are talking to in your mind."

"A man—old, sort of, but very kind. The only thing I can't ever imagine is His face."

"See, Leah. You believe. That's how I picture Heavenly Father too. And neither can I imagine His face. Now, how do you feel about Christ?"

"Well, I . . . I've always felt that He was God's Son, and I've always thought that He'd come. Only . . . only I just wish that He'd hurry!"

"So do I," Leah's mother responded gently. "But did you hear yourself, my daughter? You do not doubt His existence. You simply long for His coming, and you fear that it might not be in time to save us from tomorrow's death. Leah, you *do* have a testimony."

"Then why do I feel that I doubt?"

"Because you are mortal, and occasionally you do. We all do. But out of doubt and sincere searching for answers grows faith and, ultimately, knowledge. But Leah, during that growth process, your mortal accountability has made you susceptible to the temptations and snares of the evil one. Do you suppose he wants you to believe?"

"No, I wouldn't think so."

"Of course he doesn't. Lucifer's entire desire is to thwart the great plan and work of God. Remember, he will do *anything* to encourage our doubts. He'll use anyone he can to help him, too, including those whom we call our dearest friends. He knows that when one is lonely one is also most susceptible, and, believe me, he works on that.

"And strangely, loneliness seems to be something that comes with a testimony. That gives him a very easy entry to our souls."

"But why do we have to be lonely to be good?"

"Why don't you answer that, my daughter?"

"I don't know," Leah responded slowly. "I suppose maybe it is because so few really are."

"Lonely or good? Which do you mean?"

"Both, I suppose."

"I think you're right, my daughter. One must give up much in the way of worldly things in order to follow God, and not many are willing to do that. Those who do *are* lonely."

"Are you?"

"Very. And afraid, too. Didn't you see me shaking when those people were yelling at us?"

Leah looked at her mother in surprise. "No. In fact, I was surprised at how strong you were."

Now her mother laughed. "Good. I'm happy that I looked that way. But I wasn't. My knees were trembling, and I was scared to death. Besides, I was so lonely for your father that I wanted to cry."

"Father, is he lonely too?"

"Why of course. Haven't you noticed that?"

"No, I haven't. He seems so popular, with people

around him all the time. I rarely see him when one person or another isn't trying to speak with him or question him or seek his help. How could he ever be lonely?"

"Crowds of people do not eliminate loneliness, my daughter. Perhaps your father feels the pain of loneliness more than anyone else in the land. I know that he is carrying a burden much greater than the one you and I carry, much greater, I suspect, than either of us can understand. That burden alone makes a man lonely. And, to be honest, I feel that he needs our help and support rather than our complaints."

Leah did not reply, but as they walked she found herself thinking of that and wondering if she were indeed complaining. She also wondered, still, if she did believe, and if that would make her approaching death any easier. She couldn't imagine that it would, but still—

It was nearly sunset when Leah and her mother found the clearing in the trees where her father was praying. He was kneeling almost prostrate upon the earth, and from the occasional sobs that wracked his body, Leah knew that he was indeed suffering.

For long moments the two women watched in silence, and then Leah's mother drew her back into the trees.

"My daughter," she whispered gently, "we need to join him and add our faith to his, that his burden will not be so heavy. But first, tell me what you see."

Leah, uncertain about what she was supposed to say, shrugged. "Father is praying," she answered simply.

"Did you notice all his friends?" the woman asked.

Surprised, Leah looked up. "What?"

"The crowds you spoke of," her mother repeated. "Did you notice them?"

"Mother, he's alone. You know that."

"Does he look lonely now?"

The girl dropped her head and nodded.

Leah's mother now turned and faced her daughter. "He is, Leah, but he isn't. He is with Heavenly Father and His Son, who are the only absolutely true friends any of us will ever have. Even at a time like this they can comfort and give understanding. And they will, if we but ask as your father is doing.

"My eldest daughter, in this life we must make choices. They are ours to make, and we will reap the rewards they bring us, both good and bad. Will we follow God, or won't we? Will we stand tall even when we are alone, or will we cast our testimony aside at the first sign of opposition from those whom we call our friends?

"Leah, I have determined to follow God, and though I fear greatly and feel terribly alone, I will not waver, for to me loneliness and even death are preferable to losing the eternal companionship of your father, you, and my other children. Nor can I bear to give up my eternal reward with our God. Do you understand?"

Leah nodded silently.

"I knew you would. Now don't you think we should join your father?"

The girl stood in silence then, watching the man in the clearing but thinking of other things. "I just feel so bad about Ruth," she finally said.

"Of course you do," Leah's mother stated, her voice filled with understanding. "As do we all. And perhaps before tomorrow we can—

"Good heavens, look at your father!"

Leah looked again to the clearing and saw her father, who had suddenly risen to his feet. His face was lifted into the air, his hands were outstretched, and he was smiling . . . smiling through his tears.

Slowly he turned, saw his wife and Leah, and instantly started toward them, his face showing the most unusual expression Leah had ever seen.

Suddenly Leah felt herself thrill and begin to shake as her father drew nearer. She became aware of the light that was upon his countenance, and chills began racing up and down her spine.

He knew! Somehow this man who was her father, but whom the world knew as Nephi the prophet, had learned when . . . when—

And just as suddenly, Leah knew as well. The Spirit of God bore magnificent witness to her—

"My lovely wife and daughter," the Prophet Nephi said as he took the two women into his arms, "there is no need for worry, not for us nor for any of the Believers.

The Lord has spoken, and he has calmed my fears. Now come, we must hurry and spread the word."

"Word?" Leah asked with surprise as she stared up at her father, trying to understand. "But now is not the time for missionary work. It is—"

"Leah," her mother said softly as her own eyes suddenly grew tearful. "Look up to the heavens and behold."

Her heart hammering with joy because of what she knew she was going to see, Leah turned to the west where her mother pointed, squinted her eyes against the glare from the sun, and was startled to see that . . . that there was *no* sun there, none at all. Yet the brightness remained. In fact, it filled the sky, and once again she thrilled.

"It is the promised sign," the man called Nephi declared reverently, "the sign foretold by the dark-skinned prophet Samuel.

"He is coming.

"Tonight there will be no darkness, and on the morrow will the Son of God be born into the world. So He has declared through the centuries, and so His voice has declared again this day, even to your father.

"Leah, tomorrow is not to be a day of death, but of life, eternal life. Now come. Ere long there will be many to teach, many more than we can imagine, and the Lord would have me be about it."

Together then the three moved quickly toward the city, and Leah, again looking up, marveled and shivered anew at the brightness of the evening sky. And suddenly, as she noticed for the first time the new star that also shone from the heavens, Leah understood that her mother had been right. She did know! She had known all along, and because she knew she suddenly realized that she need never be lonely again.

From the Books of Helaman
and 3 Nephi
we discover that . . .

Of all the events recorded in scripture, it is doubtful that any
was more anxiously awaited and more eagerly looked forward
to than the birth of Jesus Christ. His coming fulfilled
prophecies that spanned approximately four thousand years,
and prophets during that time who knew him as Jehovah
longed to see the day when He would be born as Jesus, the one
who would become the Christ. Samuel, an ancient American
prophet of Lamanitish descent, was one of these. His
prophecies and their fulfillment form the basis of the preceding story.

According to the record left us by Mormon, Samuel appeared to the Nephites in the eighty-sixth year of the Reign of
the Judges, which proved to be 6 B.C.[1] He came crying repentance, as has been the role of all prophets, but he was indeed
an anomaly, for he was a Lamanite, a member of a group that
was traditionally wicked, crying repentance to the Nephites,
who had been traditionally righteous.

In the seventy-second year of the Reign of the Judges, the
prophet Nephi, sickened by the wickedness of the Nephites,
had pleaded with the Lord that a famine might come lest the
people be destroyed by the sword.[2] The Lord complied, the
famine lasted four years, and the people were humbled and
repented, and so Nephi asked the Lord that the famine end.[3]
Again the Lord complied.[4]

Righteousness continued, and by the end of the seventy-
seventh year most of the people, both Nephites and Lamanites, were member of the Church.[5] However, a secret society
called the Gadianton Robbers that had its origins at least partially among the ancient society of the Jews[6] began growing
again, and soon people were flocking to it in alarming num-
bers.[7]

The fear of this group brought many more to repentance,[8] but this was not enough. The influence of this evil body
was so strong and pervasive that by the eighty-fifth year most
of the Nephites had turned from the truth to join it, their souls
filled to overflowing with pride and wickedness.[9] In the following year the Lord sent Samuel.

Samuel's prophecies are very specific, and one wonders how such confusion and dissension arose concerning them. He prophecied first that unless the people repented, four hundred years would not pass away before the Nephites were destroyed.[10] He stated that the earth was cursed to the wicked so that their treasures and their weapons would become slippery and would vanish.[11]

He told the people that they had reached the point where they would kill all prophets except those who supported them in their wickedness.[12] He explained that they were seeking for happiness in wickedness, which thing was contrary to the nature of God.[13]

Finally he prophesied that five more years would not pass away before the Son of God would come.[14] He said that there would be great lights in heaven and that there would be no darkness for a day and a night and a day,[15] though the sun would indeed set at night and rise again in the morning.[16] He predicted that a new star would arise, such as none of them had ever seen before,[17] and that there would be many other signs and wonders in heaven.[18]

Concerning the Savior's death, he prophesied that the sun and moon and stars would be darkened for the space of three days, from the hour of his death to the hour of his resurrection.[19] He foretold thunderings, lightnings, and earthquakes.[20] He stated that the rocks over the face of the whole land, which at that time were almost one solid mass, would be broken up and fragmented and would ever after be found in seams and cracks and in broken fragments, both above and beneath the earth.[21] He spoke of great tempests[22] and explained that mountains would be made into valleys and that valleys would be thrust up into mountains.[23] He told the people that their highways would be broken up and that many of their cities would be left desolate.[24] And finally, he prophesied that many of the graves of the early Saints would be opened, and that many of them would appear to the people.[25]

The first prophet whose name was Nephi once said that the guilty took the truth to be hard, for it cut them to the very center.[26] So it was with most of the Nephites who heard Samuel. A few repented and sought baptism, but most were angry and did their best to slay the Lamanite. According to the record, however, the Lord protected his prophet, and the

stones, arrows, and spears aimed at Samuel could not harm
him.[27] Following his discourse he cast himself down from the
wall of the city and returned to his own people, and he was
never heard of more.[28]

Time passed and Samuel's prophecies began to be
fulfilled. Angels began to appear with glad tidings unto
many,[29] and by the ninetieth year of the Reign of the Judges
many signs and wonders were being seen in the heavens.[30]
Nevertheless, most of the people began to harden their hearts,
both among the Nephites and the Lamanites, and with great
intellectual convolutions they sought ways of explaining away
what they had seen and heard.[31] They reasoned mightily, stat-
ing that some things were guesswork and that others would
never happen.[32] They decided that it was easy to prophesy of
something what would happen in a distant land where it
couldn't be verified, and they declared that they were far too
intelligent to believe in such nonsense.[33] So it went, as with
modern intellectualism, seeking to reason away the power and
majesty of God. And all the while, time was passing inexorably
by.

In the ninety-first year of the Reign of the Judges, it had
been some 600 years since Lehi had left Jerusalem.[34] Nephi
the prophet and his brother Lehi had vanished, leaving the
records and other sacred things, as well as the keys of leader-
ship, with Nephi's son, whose name was also Nephi.[35] As the
ninety-second year began, there were even greater signs and
wonders.[36] The five years since Samuel's prophecy were
nearly past, and the few righteous began to look for the signs
of the Savior's birth. The unbelievers, however, declared that
the time was past,[37] and with great glee they rejoiced over the
discomfiture of the believers.[38]

One wonders today why there was a question concerning
when the five years was past, and two or three possibilities present themselves. First, perhaps no one expected that prophecy
to be so exact as it appears to have been, for the signs were apparently given five years to the day from when they were predicted. Second, maybe the people did expect it, and because
the believers set the date for the signs to be given, the unbelievers went along with them and set the same date for their
execution should the signs not appear. Finally there is evidence that Nephi the son of Helaman, who had vanished by
the time the signs were given, did not make a complete record

of Samuel's prophecy.[39] Perhaps, among other things, he forgot to date it. That would mean that no one knew of the exact date, and that they were working only from memory.

But whatever the reason, as the day for the signs approached, the righteous people found themselves in a spot. If the signs prophesied by Samuel did not appear as expected, they would all be put to death.[40]

Nephi, as one can imagine, was sorrowful about the development,[41] and so he went out and bowed himself down upon the earth in prayer, seeking for understanding.[42] He prayed almost all day,[43] and finally, late that afternoon, the voice of the Lord came to him, saying, *"Be of good cheer; for behold, the time is at hand, and on this night shall the sign be given, and on the morrow come I into the world, to show unto the world that I will fulfill all that which I have caused to be spoken by the mouth of my holy prophets."*[44]

One can easily imagine the joy with which Nephi received this news, as well as the relief the believers must have felt and the rejoicing they must have done when, with the going down of the sun, there was no darkness.[45]

The unbelievers, on the other hand, fell to the earth with fear,[46] for not only was it still light, but through that light glowed a new star,[47] exactly as Samuel had foretold. Truly it was a day to remember.

---

1. Helaman 13:1-2.
2. Helaman 11:1-5.
3. Helaman 11:10-18.
4. Helaman 11:17.
5. Helaman 11:21.
6. Lucy Mack Smith letter, *Ensign*, October 1982, pp. 70-73.
7. Helaman 11:25-30.
8. Helaman 11:34-35.
9. Helaman 11:37.
10. Helaman 13:5.
11. Helaman 13:17-19, 21, 31, 36.
12. Helaman 13:27.
13. Helaman 13:38.
14. Helaman 14:2.
15. Helaman 14:3.
16. Helaman 14:4.
17. Helaman 14:5.
18. Helaman 14:6.
19. Helaman 14:20.

20. Helaman 14:21 (see "The Witness" story and "Discovery" note for more information on Christ's death and subsequent visit to America).
21. Helaman 14:22.
22. Helaman 14:23.
23. Ibid.
24. Helaman 14:24.
25. Helaman 14:25.
26. 1 Nephi 16:2.
27. Helaman 16:2.
28. Helaman 16:7-8.
29. Helaman 16:14.
30. Helaman 16:13.
31. Helaman 16:15.
32. Helaman 16:16.
33. Helaman 16:18-21.
34. 3 Nephi 1:1.
35. 3 Nephi 1:2-3.
36. 3 Nephi 1:4.
37. 3 Nephi 1:5.
38. 3 Nephi 1:6-8.
39. 3 Nephi 23:9-14.
40. 3 Nephi 1:9.
41. 3 Nephi 1:10.
42. 3 Nephi 1:11.
43. 3 Nephi 1:12.
44. 3 Nephi 1:13.
45. 3 Nephi 1:15, 19.
46. 3 Nephi 1:16.
47. 3 Nephi 1:21.

The Conference

"Hush, my darling," the woman said gently as she lifted her tiny daughter and held her close. "In a few moments it will begin, and you must be still."

"Mother," her eldest son whispered, "how long will this last?"

"The same as yesterday," she answered, smiling down at the five-year-old boy. "You've been to conference before. Now, will you be able to care for your brother if I need to leave?"

"I did it yesterday," the boy answered proudly. "If I hold his hand, then he knows he isn't alone, and he isn't so afraid."

With a smile the woman reached out and caressed the hair of her eldest son, feeling thankful indeed that such a fine boy had been sent first to her family, especially since her second son was blind and her husband was . . . was . . .

The woman was not old, scarcely past her second score of years. In feature she was dark, a Lamanitish woman, and over the course of her life many had called her beautiful. Yet years before, a man chosen by God, a man named Samuel, had called her both pure and lovely, and those two words had set the course of her life. Her outward beauty she had little considered from that day on, concentrating instead upon the thoughts of her heart and the countenance of her eternal spirit, striving to become in actual fact the woman that the man of God had told her she was.

Not always had she been successful, of course, for she had faults, many of them. Still, she tried, and each day she set out determined to do better than the day before in the way of personal righteousness.

So she had grown both in body and in spirit, had reached the age for marriage, and had been united with a young man whom she had loved dearly and who had seemed to feel the same about her and about the things of eternity as well.

Yet after two glorious years their second son had come, entering life with sightless eyes and ears that heard nothing. For some reason her husband had become embittered over that. She, too, had struggled briefly, and then something, some trivial incident between her husband and another man who was also a member of the Lord's church, had led him into total anger and inactivity. That action had shocked *her* into repentance, but for her husband no such change had occurred. The Spirit had departed from his life, he had fallen into paths of iniquity, and finally he had even become a persecutor of those who believed. And now she and the children were alone, for he had been taken in the great destruction. Her little daughter had been born after his death and so would never know her father, and . . . Oh, how could it have happened? How was it possible that he could have—

"Mother?"

"Yes?" she answered, unconsciously drying her tears.

"Will He come today?"

"It . . . it is possible, my son. You know what the Prophet said yesterday, don't you?"

"Uh-huh. That is why we have gathered together here at the temple."

"Well, are you exercising your faith as he asked you to do?"

"I . . . I am trying, mother."

"You seem hesitant. Don't you want Him to come?"

"No . . . I mean, I do, but I want Lem to be able to see

Him too, and the men who have looked at him have not been able to restore the sight to his eyes. Maybe next time they see him . . ."

Slowly the young mother reached out and drew her eldest son close to her, while once more her tears fell freely. "Ah, my eldest son, God has indeed been good, sending me one such as you to be my firstborn in my travail. But now you must not worry. God loves all of us, *including* your sightless younger brother. He will be taken care of in the Lord's own way. Besides, it is a bright and beautiful morning, we are surrounded by good people who have much faith, and, one never knows, perhaps this will indeed be the day of His coming."

She thought of that then, wondered for perhaps the thousandth time what it would be like if the blessed event should indeed occur, and decided that she should not dwell so heavily upon the hoped-for coming. After all, it had been almost a year since the great destruction. Everyone she knew had expected His coming each and every day since then, and nothing at all had happened. Nor would it likely occur today, though deep in her heart there was the consuming desire to see—

The young woman was suddenly aware that a man was watching her, a man who had seated himself just beyond her eldest son. For an instant she was embarrassed because of her tears, but then the man smiled easily. She saw the sincerity in his face and returned his smile as best as she was able.

After several seconds of eye contact, during which the man seemed to be thinking thoughts at her, he suddenly flushed and turned the other way.

Disquieted and yet intrigued, the woman readjusted her daughter's wraps and cautiously examined the man more closely. He was also Lamanitish, seemed somewhat older than herself, was not so much good looking as he was attractive—and was alone.

Was his wife just late coming forward, she wondered instantly, or was it possible that his wife had been taken in the great destruction just as her own beloved—

And then her mind was away and she was seeing

again the fearsome storm and the terrible thunderings
and lightnings and the shakings and groanings of the
earth, and she and her husband and two sons were flee-
ing the city—only she was great with child, and slow. Her
husband was yelling and urging her to greater speed, she
was trying without much success, and, suddenly, in the
flashing brilliance from a nearby bolt of lightning, she
had seen a monstrous whirlwind appear out of nowhere
to tear her husband from her grasp.

She could still hear his horrified screaming; she could
still see the abject fear and terror in his eyes as he had
been sucked upward into the awful darkness; she
could—

"Are you not well?"

In surprise the woman spun toward the sound of the
voice and found herself gazing into the dark eyes of the
man who was seated next to her son.

"I . . . ah . . . yes . . ." she stammered. "It is only that
I was remembering the . . . the awful destruction . . ."

"It is the same with all of us," the man said quietly as
he edged somewhat closer. "Always before my eyes is the
vision of the fire that consumed our city, and of the
woman of my heart who was also consumed."

The man's eyes clouded over, and the woman found
herself aching for the pain he felt as much as for her
own.

"Was . . . was she a follower of the Prophet?" she
asked timidly, "or was she . . . No, I am sorry. I should
not have asked such a thing. I . . ."

The man regarded her closely, his expression bleak
and distant. Finally he spoke. "There is no harm done,"
he replied quietly. "Yes, she was a follower, full of faith
and very devout. But she was also gifted with words, a
wondrous leader, and when the men who governed our
new tribe came to her and offered her a position of im-
portance, she accepted immediately.

"Nor did I object, for it seemed a great honor for
both of us to have her so chosen. You see, we had no children, had never been able to, and her time was a heavy
weight upon her hands.

"In her new position the responsibilities were great, but she was gifted, and she carried them well. Her power and authority grew, and soon I feared that the things of this world had become more important to her than the riches of eternal life. I pleaded with her, but she laughed at my concern and showed me our fine home and the many comforts of our surroundings as proof of God's approval. I relaxed, and her great pride grew steadily more obvious. Finally all my prayers were for her and my own eternal well-being.

"Then came the day when with anger she told me of a foolish young man who had found his way into her place of judgment and had publicly condemned her.

"My wife was truly furious, but she spoke with joy and pride of how she had directed her guards to cast the rabble-rouser out and to teach him a lesson that he would not soon forget."

The woman gasped in fear. "And . . . and was the young man a prophet?"

"He was," the man replied quietly, "for he was speaking by the power of God. I even knew and loved him, and I knew too that the Lord had sent him among our people, along with many righteous others, to declare repentance. Yet her guards stoned him, others joined in, and he died, and though my wife declared vehemently to me that the punishment was just, from that moment on my heart knew only fear."

"Oh, there were so many of us who were taken," the woman whispered. "Some no doubt were evil, but so many of the others could have been brought back, could have . . . Oh, why did God bring all this great destruction to pass? I think and I think, and yet I do not understand at all! Nor do I understand why I was spared. I, too, have had evil thoughts. In my life there have been many times when I brought pain to others and when I did much that was unjust."

"Again," the man responded, "it is the same with all of us. I have much that I am ashamed of, and I will never understand why I was allowed to remain. But perhaps my understanding is not so important. Perhaps I need only to place my trust in God's understanding, hearken to the voice of Nephi the prophet as I strive with all my heart to keep the commandments, and wait with patience until God's will shall be made known."

The man's voice grew quiet. He and the woman both stared ahead without seeing, their thoughts elsewhere, and suddenly into the buzzing silence of the morning there came an unfamiliar sound.

Without thinking the woman rose to her feet. Still she stood, and with no more movement than tall grass on a windless day. The man and even her boys were also standing motionless. Even her restless daughter lay without movement in her arms, and the woman found an instant to realize that and to wonder at it.

Again she heard the sound that had so immobilized her just seconds before, and again she glanced about her. It was a sound that was unlike anything she had ever heard, loud and yet small, voice-like and yet piercing, so uniquely powerful that her entire body shook with the hearing of it.

Protectively the woman reached out and pulled her two sons nearer, and she was not surprised to see the man also place his arm over the shoulder of her eldest son.

All about them was absolute silence, for among the people who had gathered together for conference there existed a strange excitement, a sense of subdued wonder at what the sound might mean.

Suddenly the woman was certain she knew what was happening. Her heart leaped, her muscles began to tremble, her chest burned with a fire such as she had never experienced, and she *knew.*

Instantly she felt the strength leave her legs. She slowly dropped to her knees in humbled awe, realizing as she did that her sons and the man beside her had done the same.

And then the sound—the *voice*—came for the third time.

For a brief moment there was a quiet murmuring from the multitude, a whispering that quickly faded into

silence as the voice continued. For this time she and all
the others understood the words, words of introduction
that reverberated like thunder and the quiet whisper of
falling snow through the total stillness of the morning.

"Behold my Beloved Son," the voice declared, *"in whom I
am well pleased, in whom I have glorified my name—hear ye
him."*

In the perfect silence of the morning the young
woman lifted her eyes and gazed upward, and there she
beheld, high above her in the air, a Man. Yet such a man
she had never before seen, never before even imagined.

He was dressed in a robe of exquisite whiteness, his
hands were outstretched by way of blessing and benedic-
tion, and his face, his lovely face—

And then the young woman *knew,* with a knowledge
more sure and certain than anything she had ever before
known, with a knowledge that put all faith aside. She was
in the presence of the Son of God, the very Jesus the
Christ, He whom the prophets had declared should
come.

With motherly instinct the woman glanced at her
children and was startled to see that her second son, the
one who had been born without hearing and without
sight, was staring upward with as rapt attention as his
older brother. Then she looked at the baby in her arms,
and saw that even the tiny girl was gazing intently upward. At last she looked at the man who knelt near her,
saw the tears flowing freely from his eyes as he watched
the Being above him, and finally she realized that she was
sobbing as well.

Again she cast her tear-filled eyes heavenward, and
suddenly her pounding heart felt as if it would burst
from her body. He had drawn nearer, much nearer, and
at once she was gazing into the unbelievably radiant
countenance and piercing eyes of . . . of the Lord Jesus
Christ. In His face was such brilliance that His entire person seemed to be made of pure light, more bright than
anything she had ever before seen, more filled with light
than anything she had ever even considered.

In that face there was power, too, an awesome strength

coming from pure divine manhood that would put to
rest for all time, at least in her own mind, any idea of
weakness of any kind that might exist in the Being who
was slowly descending from above her.

More than the light, however, and even more than
the power, the thing that impressed the woman most as
she gazed reverently upward into the face of her God
and her Savior, was the sense of love, pure and unrestrained, that flowed outward and down into her own
heart and soul.

It was an amazing kind of love, astonishing in its
power and scope, and it overwhelmed her as she knelt,
gazing upward.

The young woman felt her baby daughter stir and
realized with a distant awareness that her eldest son was
tugging gently at her arm. However, she could not answer, could not even respond. She was simply too involved in the astoundingly unconditional love she was
feeling. She could not comprehend it, but neither could
she get beyond it to consider anything else about the remarkable event she was experiencing. All she could
think of was the love, the absolutely pure and unrestrained love—

Nor was it in any way critical. Somehow she understood, even as she knelt there, that Christ knew every un-
lovable thing about her, including her secret thoughts
and schemes as well as her deeds. And even with that she
was loved, totally and completely and without reservation. And that was so far beyond her mortal ability to
grasp that it was all she could think of, all she could focus
on.

And then, as Christ descended close enough so that
his eyes were visible, the woman experienced something
else, a sense of time suspended and space expanded.
Suddenly, in less time than it took to remember it, she
was shown, spread out around her in vivid and colorful
detail, one at a time and yet somehow simultaneously,
each and every event and thought and action of her life.
And somehow she also understood, in that instant of
time when all things were brought to her remembrance,

that in spite of all the love she had been given and had been blessed with since her birth, she had never truly learned to love in return.

There were, of course, incidents when she had managed to love, and these increased dramatically after her marriage and the birth of her children. But the pattern seemed to her to be otherwise, an unintentional but undeniable selfishness that now seemed to her so small, so shameful—

Suddenly the Son of God was standing on the ground before her, before all of the multitude, and as her sons put their arms around their mother, that glorious Being who was Jesus the Christ opened His mouth and . . . spoke. And His voice, even from a distance, was of such quiet and powerful clarity that it could never be characterized, could never be described. As with His love, it could be understood only by being felt.

"*Behold,*" He declared while the woman's entire frame shook with joy and awe, "*I am Jesus Christ, whom the prophets testified shall come into the world.*"

For the woman, the next few hours seemed a momentary blur, time flowing together as though none had passed and yet each of the hundreds of moments filled to overflowing with memories and sensations and feelings that she was certain she would never forget.

Especially, however, there was the moment after Christ had announced that He had given His life for them, when He invited each person present to come forward and feel His wounds with their own hands.

Never in eternity would the woman forget the shock of pain that had been hers as her fingers had explored the jagged wounds from the nails and the narrow hole where the spear had entered the Master's side. Nor would she ever again feel about sin as she had hithertofore felt. Sudden understanding gave her to know that those horrendous wounds were suffered, at least in part, because of her own weaknesses, her own shortcomings, her own sins, her own lack of love for others.

Then there had been the moment when Christ had called out the names of twelve men to be His disciples.

They were Nephi the prophet, his brother Timothy and his son Jonas, Mathoni, Mathonihah, Kumen, Kumenonhi, Jeremiah, Shemnon, Jonas, Isaiah, and Zedekiah. The woman had watched in wonder as those men, their expressions universally of stunned disbelief, had stepped forth to receive private instructions from the God who was the Savior of the world.

Later the men had returned to their places, their faces radiating light and wonder, and then she and all the vast multitude had sat together in rapt silence, listening to the powerful words of Christ.

All had wept together when, hours later, He had finished and had announced His departure. And now she sat still, stunned once again by His compassion, His unbelievable capacity to love, hoping with all her heart that her Lord would delay His departure.

Suddenly she was aware that her eldest son was shaking her hand, and so with a great effort she pulled her attention from the Master and turned to her son.

"Mother," he whispered urgently, "May I take Lem to Him? Please?"

"But . . . perhaps it would be too great an intrusion on His—"

"Sister," the man seated next to her whispered, "Christ has been good enough to promise blessings to the halt, the blind, the deaf, and all who are in any way ill. I beg of you, let the lads go."

With sudden understanding, the woman considered for the first time that Christ could, and would, heal her son. The thought, joyous as it was, brought forth new tears, and the woman buried her face in her hands.

"Do not be afraid, my friend."

"I do not cry from fear," the woman answered quickly. "I . . . I am thrilled for my Lemuel. But I worry that he won't need me so much when he is whole. I have been so lonely, so *very* lonely, especially since . . . since . . . Anyway, sometimes I think that he and the baby have been all that have saved me. Still, to think of my son as whole, I can not even imagine the joy such a blessing would be to him."

The man smiled. "I understand. And I also understand about your loneliness."

"You . . . you do?" the woman asked, looking for the
first time directly into the man's eyes.

"Yes," he responded almost in a whisper. "In fact,"
and now the man's voice dropped so low that the woman
had to strain to hear him, "I sense . . . nay, I *hope*, that
soon my loneliness will end and you will be needed more
than ever."

Questioningly, the woman looked even more deeply
into the man's eyes.

"I . . . I mean," he continued hesitantly, "that I would
like to see you . . . at least . . .well . . . in a time such as
this, where all things have changed, it is not good for . . .
for a man to be alone. Nor would I think it good for a
woman. That . . . is why I thought that perhaps, ah . . . "

Quickly the woman smiled, mostly to help the poor
man feel a little more at ease, and maybe a little to cover
the rapid beating of her own heart. She didn't understand
how she could choose such a remarkable moment to be
feeling so . . . so flustered and, well, so excited to be near
a good man, but indeed she was, and it was very obvious
that the man beside her was feeling the same way toward
her.

Perhaps later on, she found herself thinking, *after the
visit from the Lord has ended, the two of us might—*

"May . . . may I take your hand?" the man suddenly
asked.

When the woman looked startled, he hastily explained. "I mean, I would like to join my faith with
yours—in . . . in behalf of your little son. I thought if we
held hands . . . "

Gently the woman reached out and took the prof-
fered hand. They knelt and bowed their heads, and with
tears flowing freely she prayed in the name of Him who
stood before them all that her tiny Lemuel might be
healed of his afflictions.

When at last the woman finished praying, she felt a
slight squeeze. She opened her eyes to gaze into the
man's tear-streaked but kindly face, felt a mighty com-

fort from his goodness and great faith, and thought about taking her hand back—

With a wink and another squeeze, the man reached down and scooped up the deaf and blind child.

"I think it's Lemuel's turn," he said, beaming.

Quickly the lovely young woman stood. "It is," she whispered as she wiped at her fresh tears of gratitude, "Oh, it is."

"And I think," the man continued, "that you should all go forth together."

The woman smiled in agreement. Then, placing her arm through that of her new companion, she gently yet confidently spoke. "Yes, and you should come with us. Then, if it truly is your wish, as it is mine, and if it is also right in the Lord's sight, perhaps He will bless even . . . the two of us."

At first the man stared in disbelief, but then his face broke into a smile as wide as all eternity.

And thus, hand in hand with her children and the goodly man who had already been so long at her side, the young woman started forward—she and the others seeking together the blessings and the love of Jesus Christ their Lord.

From the Book of 3 Nephi we discover that . . .

When the resurrected Jesus visited the Nephites, in A.D. 34,[1] it was an unparalleled and momentous event. According to the record, it had been only a little less than a year since the signs had been given concerning the Savior's crucifixion.[2] About twenty-five hundred people[3] were gathered about the temple in the land Bountiful,[4] probably in a conference convened by Nephi the prophet,[5] discussing the momentous events they had all survived,[6] listening to discourses concerning Jesus the Christ,[7] and exercising their faith that the resurrected Lord might appear unto them.[8]

As they met together there came a voice to them that they did not understand.[9] It was a small voice, neither loud nor harsh. Nevertheless it pierced them to the center and caused their entire bodies to shake and their hearts to burn.[10] Again the voice came, again it was not understood,[11] and so the voice came the third time. Finally the multitude understood; it was an introduction by God the Father of His Beloved Son, Jesus Christ the Lord.[12]

At that point all cast their eyes upward, and all beheld a Man, dressed in a white robe, descending toward them from heaven.[13] Once upon the earth the Man stretched forth His hand and declared His identity.[14] Instantly the multitude fell to the earth, for now all the prophecies had come together and they knew of a surety of their truthfulness.[15]

Jesus then asked them to stand, and once they had done so He invited them, one and all, to come forth and feel the wounds in His hands and feet that they might know of a surety, once again, that it was indeed He. According to the record, all did.[16]

Next He called forth Nephi and gave him authority to baptize, and then He called forth the remainder of the Nephite twelve and gave them the same power.[17] Mormon in his record names all of them.[18]

Then came much teaching, which apparently took most of the day. When Jesus was finished with His discourses, in one of the most love-filled and memorable chapters in all of scripture, Jesus found himself bound to these Nephites by their pure desire for His presence.[19] Filled with compassion for these who so obviously loved Him (a direct contrast to the crowds in Jerusalem who had, only a few months before, crucified Him with hatred as much as with nails), Jesus healed the sick,[20] blessed the little children,[21] and called the people to witness as angels descended from heaven to minister to those same children.[22]

Surely for those who were there, the way to Bountiful and the temple must have been lofty with righteousness and very, very lonely. Yet without a doubt, not one of those people who had suffered and gone through so much would have changed places with anyone else, not in all of eternity.

---

1. 3 Nephi 11, footnote.
2. 3 Nephi 8:5; 11:18 (according to Mormon's record, the signs of Christ's death were given in the first month of the thirty-fourth

year, and His appearance to the Nephites came at the end of that
same year).
3. 3 Nephi 17:25.
4. 3 Nephi 11:1.
5. This is the authors' reasoning, based upon Mormon's declarations
that the people were a multitude of believers gathered at the temple
in the land Bountiful; that they were discoursing upon the changes
in the land and upon the mission of Jesus Christ; and that they were
exercising their faith both individually and collectively. These
statements sound remarkably like a modern general conference of
The Church of Jesus Christ of Latter-day Saints, held on Temple
Square in Salt Lake City.
6. 3 Nephi 11:1.
7. 3 Nephi 11:2.
8. Ether 12:7.
9. 3 Nephi 11:3.
10. Ibid.
11. 3 Nephi 11:4.
12. 3 Nephi 11:5-7 (see "The Testimony" story and "Discovery" note in
this volume for further information concerning the signs of Christ's
birth and death in America).
13. 3 Nephi 11:8.
14. 3 Nephi 11:10-11.
15. 3 Nephi 11:12.
16. 3 Nephi 11:14-15.
17. 3 Nephi 11:22 (see "The Testimony" story, "The Witness" story,
and both of their "Discovery" notes for more on one of these
twelve).
18. 3 Nephi 19:4.
19. 3 Nephi 17:5-6.
20. 3 Nephi 17:7-10.
21. 3 Nephi 17:21.
22. 3 Nephi 17:24.

The Witness

Light.

Not much, little more than a pinpoint actually, but it was there, and the old man watched it closely. Steadfastly he looked upward, his gaze clear and unwavering, his mind crowded with the things the tiny speck of light told him.

First, it had now been at least four days—four days since he had been thrown into the hole and left to die. In those four days he had neither seen nor heard from his captors, which meant that in that time he had also neither eaten nor quenched his thirst. Interestingly, he was not hungry in the least, nor was he thirsty. His lips, mouth, and throat were moist, and from his stomach there had been not so much as a murmur of complaint. In fact, he felt just as he always did. He was not uncomfortable, just pleasantly satisfied, and as usual he found that fact gratifying.

Second, the pinprick of light told him also that his friends were near and would reach him within the next two or three days. They had all agreed to meet near where he was imprisoned within seven days of their separation, and so he knew they were coming. It was just a matter of time before they arrived.

Dropping his gaze, the old man closed his eyes and leaned back against the rock, watching the afterglow from the point of light dancing across his vision. He thought again of his friends, worried briefly that they might suffer the same fate as he, and then worried no more. They were strong, had been promised protection, and could care for themselves. No, they were not the ones he need worry about.

Nor, for that matter, was he. He felt fine and had experienced no discomfort from the cruelty of his captors, nor had he experienced any agony from the days of confinement. True, he chafed a little as he thought of what he'd rather be—no, ought to be—doing. But even that caused him little worry. There was still time, more of it, in fact, than he could truly comprehend, and this captivity would be brief by comparison. Besides, there was the reason for it, hidden as yet from him but nevertheless there, as the reasons for the events of his changed life always were. So the old man trusted completely, did his best to be patient, and refused to be troubled.

No, the ones he sincerely worried about were the ones above, the men and women who had taken him captive and who had laughingly and with much hatred and mockery thrown him into the pit.

"Father," he prayed quietly while his eyes brimmed with sudden tears, "for those who have done this my heart sorrows, and I would that Thou wouldst make a way that thy humble servant might show them it is not I that has been hurt, but they.

"Of course I would rather be free than in this pit. Nevertheless, not as I will, but as Thou wilt, for I know that there is a purpose in all things, and that all things work together for good . . ."

The hours passed slowly, and to keep his mind occupied the old man thought of things long past, remembering the good and the joyous and the beautiful that had so filled his life. And that led, as it always did, to the memory of the single greatest and most glorifying experience of his long life, the event that had led, at once and finally, to his present situation.

Closing his eyes, he let his mind drift back, his thoughts focusing on the author of that memory, the

Lord Jesus Christ. Though he considered his Savior constantly, it was not often that he allowed himself the luxury of spending time in detailed reverie. Now, however, he did, and instantly the scenes in his mind were vividly brought to life.

He recalled the countenance of the Lord that day of the great change. He thought of Christ's love and the kindness that was in His eyes, and he recalled too Christ's most generous of offers. He thought of his response to that offer, hoped for but unspoken, of the Savior's perception, and of his own surprise upon learning that his friends had desired the same blessing.

Christ had granted his desires, but the man had almost not heard. His frame had been shaking so that he was nearly prostrate, his tears had been flowing unrestrained, and in his heart had been a vast gratitude he could not even utter.

That Being of light, that powerful personage who was Jesus Christ the Redeemer, the very Son of God, had cast his eyes upon him; he had understood then the love he was feeling and had committed forever to keep God's commandments, and he had suddenly felt the burden of his guilt lifted and carried away by divine forgiveness. From that instant, the man's life was no longer his own; he had given back to God his free agency; he would never again sin intentionally; he had become a servant and a follower of the Master.

Then had come the unspeakable, glorious experience wherein he and the others had been caught up and changed, and wherein they had been shown and had learned as few others had been shown and taught in all of mortal history.

And so now, in all he did, the old man tried his best to love others in the same way that Christ had loved him—unequivocably, totally, without reservation.

The sound of muffled voices coming from above him brought the old man's attention back to the situation at hand, and as he looked upward at the tiny point of light the voices grew louder and finally became distinguishable.

"Be careful," someone shouted. "Watch yourself there!"

"I am," another replied, "but so is it!"

There was coarse laughter, and then the old man heard the voice of a woman, the one whom he remembered had been the leader.

"Wait," she cried. "Don't do it yet. The old fool may very well be dead already. If so, this would be a terrible waste."

"You're right," another shouted, a man this time. "This is the largest, most vicious one we've ever captured. No sense wasting it on a dead man. You there! Remove the cover, and we shall soon see what five days without food and drink have done to the old man."

Five days, the man thought quickly. *Then I must have missed one. Perhaps the fall caused me greater forgetfulness than I supposed. Ah, but I have felt nothing in the way of pain, so perhaps it is the way of my new life, where days fade into nothingness, and time means less and less—*

With a heavy, grating sound the trapdoor above him slid open, and as the old man squinted against the glare, he heard and even felt the movement of several people as they crowded around the hole to stare downward.

"See anything?" one asked.

"No, it's too dark. I . . . wait a minute! There he is!"

"Dead?"

"No," another answered with surprise. "See him sitting there on that boulder?"

There was a chorus of assent, and the old man, his eyes growing quickly accustomed to the light, looked up and smiled.

"Greetings," the old man said gently. "I salute you with love."

"Would you look at that?" a man declared with wonderment. "He's smiling. He doesn't even look hungry."

"Old man," another called, "are you enjoying yourself, preaching to the rocks? Do you love them as well?"

"I do," the man replied softly. "At least the rocks are obedient to our God, and they listen without mockery."

At that there was much vulgar laughter, and then the

woman, the one who seemed to be the leader, hissed viciously into the hole. "I hope you've enjoyed their silence fully, old man, for no longer will you be alone with the stones of the earth."

There was more laughter, but the woman ignored it. Rising from the hole she turned and issued quick instructions, and within seconds the others vanished from sight. The old man, still gazing upward, was aware of movement, of instructions and directions, and of muttered oaths. There was also another sound, not human, and briefly he wondered. But then the opening was partially covered with netting, and, still watching, he understood.

There was a flurry of movement, vicious hissing and snarling, and suddenly the netting parted and a writhing creature plummeted with an angry growl to the floor of the pit.

"Now, old man," the woman laughed evilly, "here is a companion for you that will most certainly end your loneliness."

Everyone laughed in appreciation of her delightful joke, but with a disdainful wave of her hand the woman silenced them. "Perhaps," she continued scornfully, "you might even win a convert to your insane rantings. Truly, however, I think it more likely that you will be converted to his."

There was another chorus of loud laughter. Then the heavy door grated back into place, and the old man was once more shut up in the dimness of the pit.

"Oh Great Father," he prayed softly, groaning, "what can one man do in the way of softening their hearts? I ache for them. Yet they have become so hard, so filled with anger, that the words of gentleness that thou taught us no longer reach them. Ah, if only I could get their attention—"

And then, for the first time, the old man became aware of the great cat that now crouched menacingly on the far side of the pit.

In the dim light its eyes glowed, and each breath it took was a snarl of hatred. Suddenly the old man saw that the black-tipped tail of the huge feline was twitch-

ing, back and forth, back and forth, giving fair warning
that it was about to spring.

For the briefest part of a moment the man shrank
backward, a carryover from his days of fear. But then his
mind was filled with something else, a definite understanding, and again he felt that all-encompassing love
the Lord Jesus Christ had held out to him.

The great cat, he suddenly understood, was injured.
Not with evil, as he had been on that day of the Savior's
coming, but with a physical wound that was almost as
painful. Perhaps it had been hurt in the fall, or perhaps
it had sustained an injury when it was captured. But no
matter when. The important thing was that it had been
hurt, and the old man's heart, filled with the pure love of
Christ, went suddenly and completely out to the snarling
creature before him.

"My furry brother," he said softly as he raised his
wrinkled hand, "you are hurt. Let me look, and I will
give you what assistance I can."

The creature made no move, save to increase the
speed with which it lashed its tail back and forth, and so
the old man stretched out his hand even farther.

"Dear Father above," he prayed, his voice still low
and gentle, "this Thy creation is injured, and I would do
for it what Thy Son would do were He here. Yet I cannot, for its heart is filled with fear. Speak to it, O Father.
Touch it with Thy love, that it might know I mean it no
harm. Then I will do for it what Thou wouldst have me
do."

The old man waited, watching closely, and gradually
the swishing tail slowed and at last was still. Only then did
the man rise and move slowly forward, his face calm and
composed, his eyes saying even more eloquently than
words how much he loved the great cat he was approaching.

"My wild brother," he said as at last he knelt beside
the quivering feline, "I will touch you now, but it will not
bring you pain. I look for injuries, that and no more."

Gently he placed his old hand on the animal's back
and held it still while the taut muscles rippled and shook

beneath his touch. The cat turned its head quickly and
bared its fangs, and from deep within its chest came a low
rumble.

At that the old man smiled with understanding, and
silently he once more told the cat of his love and respect
and of his intention to help. For a long moment the great
yellow eyes burned into his, and then the cat turned away
and the quivering in its muscles began to slow.

Only when the shaking had at last grown still did the
man's fingers begin to explore. Carefully he felt down
the big cat's side, under its belly, and down both legs
nearest him.

Nothing.

Next he explored the other side, the one across from
him, reaching around the cat and feeling carefully for
broken or bruised ribs. Finally his hand moved down the
right rear leg and then the fore one, and it was there that
the muscles twitched again, telling him that he had
found what he was looking for.

"Ah, my brother," he said as he caressed the leg, "I
fear that it is broken, for I feel the ends of the bone. Now
I must walk around you, and you must trust. That will be
difficult, and I understand why, for never has man been
your friend. Nevertheless, I am, and I cannot help you
until you are upon your side with your paw in my lap.

"Here. I will help."

And the old man, his hand never leaving the cat's
body, moved within inches of the gaping jaw and knife-
like teeth as he passed around to the other side of the
still-crouched lion. Once there he leaned into the shoulder and side of the creature, and, slowly, carefully, he
applied pressure. And while he did he quietly spoke of
his sorrow for the pain the animal was experiencing, of
his admiration for its great courage, and of his love for its
God-given spirit.

Gradually the big cat relaxed and then slowly it lay
down. When that was accomplished, the old man smiled
and began to methodically caress the injured leg, praying quietly to his Father as he did so.

At first there was no change, but then the man felt the

ends of the bone pull back from the muscles against
which they had been pressed. He continued to rub, and
soon the cat seemed to sigh, and its luminous eyes drifted
closed. Once, moments later, they opened, and the creature stared up into the face of the old man, much as if to
give thanks. Then they closed again, and soon the animal
was asleep.

"Father," the man prayed as he finally stopped rub-
bing and carefully lifted the animal's great head into his
lap, "once again I thank Thee for honoring the words
that I have uttered, however unworthily.

"Now bless this creature, I pray, that anger and
cruelty might never again be part of its life."

Two days later the door above the old man grated
open once more, and again the people laughed until
their eyes grew accustomed to the darkness below. Then,
as they saw the man seated on the same rock as before,
with his hand resting on the lion's head, they fell back in
surprise and fear.

"It's not possible," the woman gasped. "It can't be
so!"

"Maybe what they say is true," a man said. "Maybe
they cannot . . ."

"They warned us," another added, his voice nearly
hysterical. "They told us it would do no good! Aye, we
are dead . . ."

"Silence," the woman whispered hoarsely. "The old
fool is no more than us, and all who say so lie! No one can
live for more than three hundred years! All men die,
even this one. Bring the fire, and I will show you!"

Seconds later a burning brand dropped over the lip
of the pit and plummeted to the floor. The cat snarled
and pulled quickly back, but the old man caressed the
animal and spoke quietly, and gradually the animal grew
still.

Another snapping and flaming brand quickly followed, then another and another, and soon the entire
floor of the pit was deep with leaping flames. As the
brands continued to fall the old man raised his eyes. His
lips moved, and slowly he rose to his feet. Then, with his

hand still caressing the great cat, he looked deeply into its beautiful luminous eyes.

"My friend," he said as he rubbed easily behind the cat's tufted ears, "you see, it is all right. They cannot harm us. Now I thank you for your trust and companionship. You have greatly eased the hours of my waiting. I sense, however, that those with whom I labor are coming. Therefore, my furry and fearless brother, it is time for you and me to leave."

Looking up at the wall of stone, the old man raised his right hand, spoke quietly, and then without hesitation started forward, walking through the fire and directly toward the entombing stone. And without hesitation the big cat followed, seemingly as confident as the man.

Suddenly there was a deep rumble from within the earth, and as the man and the beast moved toward the wall, the rocks parted asunder with a groan that seemed almost one of relief. To the smoke from the fire was added an immense quantity of dust, but quickly it cleared away, revealing a pathway that led easily upward. In silent dignity the two started upward, and moments later they emerged unscathed from the dark and fiery bowels of the earth.

Smiling, the man leaned over, pressing his cheek against the soft whiskers of the cat's face. He blessed the animal, then straightened and watched quietly. The huge feline looked up at him, hesitated briefly, caressed his old hand with its rough tongue, and then turned and faced the terrified ones who had been its captors. Then, with a low growl, it sat on its haunches and waited.

Only then did the old man turn to face the two smiling men who waited behind him.

"My brothers," he said happily as he held out his hands toward them, "it is good that you are here. Our brothers and sisters of this place have great need of the message we have been commanded to bear."

The old man paused, looked at the cat and at his former captors who were cringing in terror from its quiet but baleful stare, and then with a righteously mischievous twinkle in his eye he turned back to his companions and continued.

"Then too, the Master has provided an ally here who can perhaps be of great help. See how the people give him their undivided attention?"

The two friends nodded seriously and stepped forward to stand beside the old man and the great cat. Then gently, with pure love flowing from their eyes in the same manner that it had once flowed from the Master to them, the three, with the silent help of the great and gentle cat, began to teach the crowd.

From the
Book of 3 Nephi
we discover that . . .

Sometime after Jesus had appeared to the Nephites and chosen His twelve disciples, and after He had watched them and had spent some time with them, He gave them a special blessing wherein He allowed them to ask whatsoever they would of Him. Nine immediately asked to be allowed to serve until they had reached the age of man, at which point they would die and return to Him.[1]

Next He turned to the three who had remained silent and asked of them their desires. They feared to answer Him,[2] but Christ knew their hearts and told them that they had desired the same thing as the Apostle John had requested in the land of Palestine.[3] Then He granted the three their desire, which was that they should never taste death but be allowed to remain on earth in His ministry and service until His return.[4]

Jesus then specified some unusual conditions under which they would live, and Mormon later verifies that each of these conditions were met in exactness. He told them that they would have no pain nor sorrow save for the sins of the world.[5] He told them that prisons could never hold them,[6] and He promised them as well that pits could not be dug deep enough to hold them.[7]

He explained that fire would never harm them.[8] He told

them that they would have the power to play as children might with poisonous serpents and wild beasts.[9] He promised that Satan could not tempt them, nor could the earth have power over them.[10] He showed them that they would be in the world but not known for who they were,[11] and He told them that if they but prayed they could show themselves to whomever they desired.[12] Finally, He gave them power to spend from that day forward in declaring His gospel.[13]

At that point Jesus touched the nine, and then the three who were left were caught up into heaven.[14] We don't know all that occurred there, but Mormon tells us that a change was wrought upon their bodies that was less than a resurrection but significantly more than most of us will experience here in mortality.[15] He also tells us that they were able to obtain that promise of Christ's only because of their exceeding great faith.[16]

Time passed, the nine disciples passed away and went to their reward,[17] and for the next hundred and thirty years peace continued. But finally selfishness crept in among the people. False churches sprang up, and one of those churches began to persecute and try to kill the three disciples who had been allowed to tarry.[18] Gradually people grew more prideful and wicked, and within another hundred years Mormon tells us that almost without exception the people, both Nephites and Lamanites, had become evil.[19] From that time forward the three disciples began to sorrow for the sins of the world.[20]

Finally, in approximately A.D. 322, the people had grown so wicked that the Lord took his three choice ones out of their midst.[21]

Little is known of these men after that. Mormon and Moroni both knew them well.[22] Moroni tells us that in his day they were the only ones in the entire land who knew the Lord,[23] and Mormon was about to reveal their names until he was spiritually constrained.[24]

Beyond this, we know only that these three are still on their missions; that at least one of them visited with Joseph Smith; that they are spoken of fondly and sadly, even apocalyptically by some Latter-day Saints who do not truly believe in them; that they are known today as the Three Nephites; that they are still doing their best to prepare the world for the return of the Savior; and that they definitely have chosen for themselves the loftiest and perhaps most lonely of ways.

1. 3 Nephi 28:2.
2. 3 Nephi 28:5.
3. 3 Nephi 28:6.
4. 3 Nephi 28:7-8.
5. 3 Nephi 28:9-10.
6. 3 Nephi 28:19; 4 Nephi 1:30.
7. 3 Nephi 28:20.
8. 3 Nephi 28:21; 4 Nephi 1:32.
9. 3 Nephi 28:22; 4 Nephi 1:33.
10. 3 Nephi 28:39-40.
11. 3 Nephi 28:27-28.
12. 3 Nephi 28:30.
13. 3 Nephi 28:29.
14. 3 Nephi 28:12-18.
15. 3 Nephi 28:37-40.
16. Ether 12:17.
17. 4 Nephi 1:14.
18. 4 Nephi 1:29-34.
19. 4 Nephi 1:43.
20. 4 Nephi 1:44.
21. Mormon 1:13; 8:10.
22. Mormon 8:11.
23. Mormon 8:10.
24. 3 Nephi 28:25-26.

The Missionary

Slowly the young missionary dropped his head, and when at last he spoke there was an anger in his voice that he could not hide. "I'm quitting," he said sullenly. "I don't like it, I'm not doing any good to anyone, and I want to go home!"

In the heavy silence that followed, the young man continued to stare at the earth, fearing the reprisal he was certain was coming and yet defiantly determined to stand up to it. Instead, however, the older man who sat before him did not lecture, did not condemn. He simply asked for help, and the young man was so startled by it that at first he could not answer.

"I think I understand," the older man finally repeated, "but could you give me your reasons before you go?"

Quickly the young man looked up. "Reasons?" he asked. "I would think they are obvious enough."

"Perhaps, but I would like to hear them from you."

"But why?"

Slowly the man sat back and took hold of his knee, formulating his response. "There will be others who will labor in this work," he finally answered, "and perhaps if I can warn them of what you have experienced, they will be more prepared."

"Prepared for what? To not be the failure I have been?"

"Do you think of yourself as a failure?"

"I must be! As far as I can tell, I haven't accomplished a single worthwhile goal since I left the Training Center. Don't *you* call that failure?"

Carefully the man regarded the youth who sat before him, realizing once more that he was speaking with one who was little more than a boy. He had known that all along, yet still the young man had been called, and it was no light matter to renounce the calling. Somehow, as the one who had been asked to preside, he had to help this young man understand that. Somehow he had to help the youth understand that his experiences were not usual nor even bad, but were instead good experiences that were simply difficult and painful to bear. But how? What could he say that would motivate, that would inspire? And above all, how could he get the boy to listen to *him?* That was the key question, and he knew it.

"Well?" the boy repeated. "Is that what you are trying to prepare others against? Failure? Because if it is, it won't work! No one is going to have success here. These people are totally evil, and no amount of preaching will ever do any good, no matter *who* does it!"

"Failure is not what I had in mind," the man answered quietly. "Endurance is what I hope to teach to other missionaries. Endurance and dedication. I hope to help each of them to accept the divinity of their calling with faith and courage and endure to the end. That will be success enough. Now what can you tell me?"

"To begin with," the boy replied defiantly, "I can tell you that I didn't fail! I can also endure. I choose not to because it is a complete waste of my time. These people don't care about truth and righteousness. They aren't interested in the gospel, nor are they interested in salvation. Why, no one has successfully preached the gospel to them in years. The entire course of these people's lives is toward wickedness, and my beating on their doors and getting driven immediately away isn't going to change that at all.

"No, I'm quitting because I'm tired of the uselessness of it. I'm tired of casting my pearls before swine, and I want to get on about my own life!"

"How long have you been here?" the man then asked.

"You know," the youth answered quickly with a slight edge of sarcasm in his voice. "I came with you, almost three months ago."

"Three months," the man repeated to himself as he tried desperately to remember how long three months had seemed when he had been young. "Three months. And in all that time, have you had any success?"

The youth laughed bitterly. "None," he answered. "Not only have I had no success, but on two or three occasions I have been lucky to escape with my life. I tell you, these people are thoroughly evil, and I want no more to do with them."

The man looked intently into the face of the youth. He had been unaware of the danger this boy had been in, at least specifically, and he felt his own heart contract with the fear of possibly losing him.

"Are you afraid?" he finally asked, doing his best to still his own fear for the life of the boy.

The young missionary dropped his eyes. "A little," he finally answered. Then quickly he continued so that the man wouldn't think him a coward. "But even then I'd stay. I'd stay in a minute if I only knew I was doing some good."

"Perhaps that is not for you to know," the older man stated quietly.

"What do you mean?"

"I mean that God in his wisdom does not tell his children all things."

"Why doesn't He? Especially when I . . . I mean we, are giving up so much to serve him."

"I'm not certain I know the answer to that," the man answered quietly. "I have some ideas, but that's all they are, ideas. I have learned, though, that God frequently expects obedience based upon faith rather than knowledge, even when such obedience without understanding leads to great pain and personal sacrifice."

"That doesn't sound like the God of love that I worship," the boy declared. "I can't imagine that He would want His righteous children to suffer!"

"Can't you?" the man replied, smiling. "If I could show you that He frequently asks for service that entails suffering, and that much good comes from obedience to such requests, would you reconsider your decision to leave?"

Slowly the boy rose to his feet and walked to the doorway, where he stood looking out. "I don't know," he replied at last. "My mind is pretty well made up. Besides, if He wants me to suffer, why doesn't He warn me in advance so that I can be ready?"

Instead of answering, the man leaned back and asked another question.

"Do you love the Lord?" he gently queried.

"Of course I do. And He loves me. That's why—"

"That's why you must listen," the man interrupted, his voice filled with the sudden power of inspiration. "Perhaps He loves you enough to spare you the responsibility of the knowledge you demand."

"What—"

"Suppose you knew that you would labor here for exactly six years, three days, and eleven minutes, present the gospel of Jesus Christ to only nine people, and convert none of them. How would you respond to that?"

"Then it would be certain that I would go home today!"

"But what if every one of those nine people needed to hear your testimony before they could stand before the bar of God and be judged with a righteous judgment?"

"I don't know . . . I . . ."

"Or, suppose you knew that in exactly thirty-three months and two hours from the time you left home, while you were teaching and before your words had been accepted by anybody, your life would be taken? How would that knowledge affect the decision you have made today?"

The young man looked quickly at the floor, his hesitation and indecision obvious.

"Do these questions give you a sense of why God quite often hides knowledge from us?

"Now sit down, my son," the older man continued, "and hear me out. I wish to tell you of another missionary, one who lived long ago, but one who had feelings and an experience similar to your own. I feel certain that once you think of his work in terms of obedience without complete understanding, you will see things quite differently. Will you listen?"

For a moment the eyes of the boy and the man locked, but at last the youth nodded and slowly took his seat. Only then did the man begin.

"Many years ago," he recounted, "the voice of the Lord came into the mind of a man whose name was Abinadi, commanding him to go to the people who were his neighbors, serve as a missionary to them, and declare unto them their great wickedness.

"Abinadi no doubt hesitated, and perhaps he even feared, for he was a busy man with much in the way of personal affairs that needed doing. Besides, he knew the people, knew of their evil ways, knew of the terrible wickedness of their king and his priests, knew of the danger he would be in, and knew too the hopelessness of his task.

"Nevertheless he girded up his loins, bowed his will to that of the Lord, went with fear and trembling before the people, and delivered his terrible message of warning.

"And, Elder, he had been right in his fears. No one listened. *No one.* Not only that, but they who heard him were wroth and rose up in their anger to destroy him.

"Abinadi prudently fled, and the Lord in his mercy delivered him out of the hands of the people.

"Still, Abinadi had stirred up a hornet's nest of anger. His words were reported to the king, whose name was Noah, and Noah, in his great wickedness, ordered Abinadi's arrest and death. From then on Abinadi was hunted relentlessly, and it must have taken all his energies and wits to avoid being captured. Yet, somehow, through two years of angry searching, he did.

"Now, with that sort of non-success behind him, Abinadi's calling must have seemed just as inconclusive to him as yours apparently has to you. And, just like you, he probably questioned why."

"But why would he question it?" the young man asked. "Didn't you say that the Lord had spoken to him?"

"Yes," the man responded, "but most likely in his mind, my son. Only in his mind. Do you suppose that feels much different from a strong or compulsive idea generated by oneself? You at least were called by one with authority traced directly back to the Lord Jesus Christ, and tangible hands were laid upon your head to give you his power. Abinadi had none of that. Tell me, which would you prefer, a strong feeling or tangible evidence?"

The young man remained silent, and so the man continued. "And as to the good he was doing, Elder, Abinadi had seen no evidence whatsoever that anything good was coming from his courageous waste of time. No one had listened, no one had even expressed interest. All he had encountered during his entire mission was hostility and hatred. Would that discourage you, do you think?"

Again there was silence.

"I imagine it even discouraged him," the man continued gently. "The entire experience must have been terribly frustrating to the lonely man who, because of his righteousness, had so suddenly been thrust into the role of a prophet.

"Anyway, probably just as the situation was settling enough so that Abinadi could get on with his own personal affairs, the word of the Lord came once more into his mind. He was called to go again before his same neighbors and proclaim an even more powerful message of repentance."

"But that . . . that isn't fair!"

"Perhaps it doesn't seem to be, but nevertheless it happened."

"I don't understand."

"Neither did Abinadi, my son, and perhaps that is the whole point of what I am trying to tell you. Abinadi *didn't* understand, and, so far as we know, the Lord didn't fill him in on any details. He simply sent him forth to do more work and expected him to have faith until understanding finally came.

"You see, Abinadi's thoughts are not recorded, but it is not difficult to imagine the hesitation he might have felt. After all, his success record up to that point was pretty clear. I would guess that he even considered quitting and going home."

"I know how he felt," the youth replied quietly.

"I think you do," the man responded. "And like you also, Abinadi seemed to fear this second call."

"Why do you think that?"

"Because once he decided to go, he wore a disguise when he went before the people."

"A disguise?"

"That is right. A disguise. Hoping against hope that his second effort might meet with a little more success, Abinadi donned a disguise and went forth, sensing, I am sure, that his feeble attempt to conceal his identity would be superfluous once he opened his mouth.

"And sadly, if those were his thoughts, he would most assuredly have been right. Not long after he had declared his message he was taken by the people, bound, and delivered into the hands of King Noah. Noah had him imprisoned, questioned his priests concerning him, and then at their suggestion brought Abinadi forth to be questioned by them all.

"And now, my son, the faith and courage of this man becomes truly evident. Noah's priests' first question was concerning missionary work, for they asked what Isaiah had meant when he had said, 'How beautiful upon the mountains are the feet of him that bringeth good tidings.'

"Such a question must have stirred Abinadi's heart, for of all the questions they might have asked him, that one dealt most specifically with his own uncertainty, with the 'why' of his being called as a missionary to such a stiff-necked people as his neighbors had become.

"He knew that he had been called of God, and that he

would be declared beautiful by the Lord only if he delivered his good tidings of peace and salvation, as well as the warnings the Lord had delivered to him. And, interestingly, he must also have realized at that moment that it mattered little whether or not those he spoke to listened. What mattered was that he declare the message in purity. The Lord, through the power of his mighty Spirit, would take care of the rest.

"Apparently taking heart from that understanding, Abinadi responded boldly and with great courage to their questions, denouncing their wickedness and waxing eloquent in his testimony of the goodness and mercy of God.

"Such forceful righteousness was dangerous, however, for it brought upon him the full wrath of King Noah, who angrily ordered Abinadi's death.

"Now, suppose you were Abinadi, my son. At that point, what would you have done?"

The young man hesitated, turned away, and at last shook his head. "I don't know," he answered quietly. "I just don't know. The courageous thing, of course, would be to die honorably. But why? Why? It doesn't seem right to die for nothing."

"I think you are right," the man responded, "and I think I know you well enough to feel certain that you would have done exactly as Abinadi did.

"Of course he did not submit and die for nothing. No one of us should. Prompted by the Spirit, he defied those evil men. 'Touch me not,' he ordered, 'for God shall smite you if ye lay your hands upon me.'

"Courage, Elder? Seldom has there been shown more. Captive and in bondage, Abinadi stood valiantly before that court and with ringing voice delivered the message God had commanded him to declare. And as he spoke, the Spirit of the Lord was upon him, and his countenance shone with an exceeding luster so that neither Noah nor his priests dared lay their hands upon him.

"And thus those wicked men were forced to listen as Abinadi taught them the fine points of the gospel and

declared to them the future mission and eternal divinity
of the Lord Jesus Christ. Nor was it a short sermon, but
lengthy, and it adhered with exactness and in all points
to the message the Lord had placed in his mind.

"When at last he had finished there was silence, and
wonder of all wonders, into that silence stepped a young
man, one of the priests. To Abinadi's surprise and probably great surge of hope, that young man began to plead
for the prophet, arguing that Abinadi be listened to and
allowed to depart in peace.

"My son, like you, Abinadi had not been told by the
Lord of his future. He had been told only that he must
needs go and preach, and that he would be blessed for
doing so. Abinadi had faith in that promise, for he was
an obedient man, and he even declared to Noah and the
others that if they should decide to take his life, then so
be it. They would one day die in a like manner.

"Still, he no doubt felt some hesitation in the face of
death, for he was a man like all of us. That is one of the
reasons why I suppose the words of the young priest
must have sounded so sweet to him.

"Sadly, perhaps, Noah was only more wroth, and he
ordered not only Abinadi's death but the young priest's
as well. The priest then made a daring escape and went
into hiding. But Abinadi, who may have sensed all along
that death would ultimately come of his efforts, but who,
so far as we know, was never explicitly told, was forced to
suffer death by fire.

"Now Elder, you have asked, and fairly, why. Why
should a man waste his time, and perhaps even his life,
declaring the gospel of Christ to those who will not listen? Abinadi, who knew only about obedience to divine
command when he suffered death, perhaps asked the
same question. And though I do not know even a small
portion of the reasons God must have for requesting
such obedience, I do know a little about the results of
Abinadi's mission. Would you care to hear them?"

Hesitantly the young man nodded, and so he who
presided began again to unfold the scriptures.

"The young priest who heard Abinadi," he explained,

"was named Alma. He was converted by Abinadi's words, and though he was powerless to save the prophet's life, he recorded the man's prophecies and taught them to others. A church was organized with Alma as its leader, and ultimately Alma's son, Alma the Younger, accepted the gospel, continued the record begun by his father, and became the Prophet.

"Alma the Younger's son Helaman kept the records after his father, passing them finally to his brother Shiblon. Shiblon gave them in turn to Helaman the son of his brother Helaman, and that Helaman gave them to his son Nephi who was the brother of Lehi, named by their father after righteous men so that they too would seek righteousness.

"Nephi passed the gospel and the records on to his son Nephi, and that Nephi, along with his son Jonas and his brother Timothy (whom he had raised from the dead), were called by Jesus Christ as disciples at the time of the resurrected Lord's visit to our land.

"That latest Nephi finally gave the records and his testimony of the Lord to his son Amos, which Amos I am.

"My son, you too are called Amos, for you have been given my name by your mother and me in the hope that you will feel as we do about the great work that you and I and the others have been called to do. For indeed, Amos, you have been called, and the records my father gave me are one day to be entrusted to you, if you are worthy, giving you the honor and responsibility of preserving the great and wondrous things of God.

"And, Elder, in a strange and wonderful way, we owe it all, you and I and your mother and your younger brother Ammaron and many thousands of others, to that lonely man called Abinadi who must surely have died wondering, even as you and I have wondered today, why he had been called to suffer through such a useless and painful mission. Now do you understand?"

In silence the young elder nodded. Then, somewhat awkwardly, he arose and embraced his father. And through the tears that followed, he said that which his father had waited so long to hear.

"How . . . how beautiful upon the mountains," the youth declared slowly, "are the feet of him that bringeth good tidings, of him who is obedient, even when he does not fully understand why. Yes, I understand, my father, and I am ready."

From the Books of Mosiah, Alma, and 3 and 4 Nephi we discover that . . .

Historically, almost nothing is known about the backgrounds of the three principal characters in the preceding story. Abinadi appears suddenly on the scene when he is called by God in some direct but unspecified manner[1] to declare repentance to his own people.[2] To his credit he did so in such a forceful manner that the people were angry and sought to take away his life.[3] However, God delivered him from their hands[4] and he went into hiding.

For two years King Noah searched for Abinadi so that he might slay him.[5] Then the call from God came to Abinadi again, and disguising himself[6] for reasons never given, he once more went forth to powerfully declare the word of God to his neighbors.[7]

Again the people were angry, but this time their efforts at capturing the prophet were successful.[8] He was taken immediately to Noah,[9] who cast him into prison.[10]

Then Noah, in conference with his wicked priests, determined to bring Abinadi forth that he might be questioned, tripped up, judged, and condemned according to his own contradictions.[11]

This was done, but the first question the priests asked regarding the meaning of the scripture we now know of as Isaiah 52:7[12] opened the door for Abinadi, and his answer to the priests was more powerful and more denunciatory than ever.[13] This so angered Noah that he ordered Abinadi's death.[14] But the prophet, filled with the Spirit of God until his face shown,[15] withstood them.[16]

Then, speaking with the power and authority of God,[17]

Abinadi unfolded the scriptures and delivered a lengthy and involved message about Christ's future mission and atonement.[18]

Finally finished and with his divine protection at an end, the prophet stood quietly as Noah commanded the priests to take him and put him to death.[19] At that point a young priest named Alma, who had recognized the truth of Abinadi's accusations, stepped forward and pleaded for the prophet's life.[20] This further angered the king, who then ordered Alma's death as well.[21] Alma fled hastily and made his escape,[22] and Abinadi was escorted back to prison.

For three days the prophet waited while charges were concocted against him,[23] and then he was taken and burned to death, valiantly continuing to deliver his message even until his last breath.[24]

Alma, meanwhile, had recorded all of Abinadi's words,[25] and now he set out secretly to teach them to his friends and neighbors.[26] He had fairly quick success, and before long he had baptized 204 souls in a pool called the Waters of Mormon.[27] Shortly thereafter the Church was organized,[28] and for the next sixty years Alma was at its head.

Upon Alma's death, in about 92 B.C., the records were given to his son who was also named Alma and was known as Alma the Younger.[29] He had sometime previously been ordained as the High Priest by his father.[30] Some nineteen years later Alma passed the priesthood and the records to his eldest son, whom he had named Helaman.[31] Helaman presided for sixteen years before he passed the records to his next younger brother, Shiblon,[32] and because Corianton, Alma's third son, had taken a ship northward out of the land and could not be reached,[33] Shiblon on his deathbed four years later gave the records to Helaman the son of his older brother.[34]

Helaman the son of Helaman kept the records for fourteen years before he passed them on to his eldest son, whose name was Nephi.[35] Nephi and his brother Lehi walked in righteousness, and Nephi kept the records for the next thirty-nine years. Finally, in the year when it was recorded that the people had been six hundred years away from Jerusalem,[36] and just prior to the time when the signs were given by God announcing Christ's birth, Nephi gave the records to his son who was also Nephi, and then he simply vanished.[37]

From then onward until the Savior's visit in A.D. 34, the

younger Nephi kept the records. In that year he was called by the resurrected Lord as one of the twelve disciples,[38] and his son Jonas and his brother Timothy were also called.[39]

At some point prior to A.D. 60, Nephi the disciple of Christ passed the records on to his son Nephi,[40] who was the third Nephi in succession to hold the records and other sacred items. That Nephi kept the records for seventy-six years before passing them on to his son Amos, the presiding authority in the preceding story, in about A.D. 111.[41] Amos kept them eighty-four years, until about A.D. 195, before passing them on to his son who was also called Amos.[42]

By then the righteousness that had prevailed since the coming of Christ was dwindling, all manner of Lamanites and other 'ites' were springing up in various political divisions, and before many more years had passed away there were few left who could be called righteous.[43] It was in that setting that Amos and his sons Amos and Ammaron apparently did their best to declare repentance and the word of God.[44] However, the experience between Amos and his eldest son that is described in the preceding story is purely fictional conjecture. There is no indication in the scriptures that it ever occurred. We wrote the story simply to show that there has indeed been precedence for discouragement, and that much good can come from even very tiny successes.

In approximately A.D. 306, Amos the son of Amos died, passing the records to his younger brother Ammaron.[45] Ammaron maintained the records as long as he could, but the general wickedness of the people had become so bad that in about A.D. 320 he was constrained by the Holy Ghost to hide the records so that they would not be destroyed.[46]

At about that same time, Ammaron went to Mormon, who was then a child of ten (and apparently unrelated to Ammaron), and gave him a charge that when he was twenty-four years old he should go to the land Antum and to a hill there called Shim, for in that hill the sacred records were concealed. At that time he was to take only the plates of Nephi and leave the others hidden. On those plates he was to engrave all the things he had seen in his youth of his people and their ways.[47]

Mormon did so, and the result of his and his predecessors' obedience and adherence to the loftier way, all the way back to the great Abinadi, is the volume of scripture now known as the Book of Mormon.

1. Mosiah 11:20.
2. Ibid.
3. Mosiah 11:26.
4. Ibid.
5. Mosiah 11:27-29.
6. Mosiah 12:1.
7. Ibid.
8. Mosiah 12:9.
9. Ibid.
10. Mosiah 12:17.
11. Mosiah 12:18.
12. Mosiah 12:21-24.
13. Mosiah 12:25-37.
14. Mosiah 13:1.
15. Mosiah 13:5.
16. Mosiah 13:2-4.
17. Mosiah 13:6.
18. Mosiah 13:7–16:5.
19. Mosiah 17:1.
20. Mosiah 17:2.
21. Mosiah 17:3-4.
22. Ibid.
23. Mosiah 17:5-6.
24. Mosiah 17:13-20.
25. Mosiah 17:4.
26. Mosiah 18:1-7.
27. Mosiah 18:14-16.
28. Mosiah 18:17.
29. Mosiah 29:11-20 (see "The Identified" story and "Discovery" note in this volume for more information on the conversion of Alma the Younger).
30. Mosiah 29:42.
31. Alma 37:1-47.
32. Alma 63:1-2.
33. Alma 63:10.
34. Alma 63:11-13.
35. Helaman 3:37.
36. 3 Nephi 1:1.
37. 3 Nephi 1:1-3.
38. 3 Nephi 11:18-21.
39. 3 Nephi 11:22; 19:4 (see "The Witness" story and "Discovery" note in this volume for more on Christ's Nephite disciples).
40. 4 Nephi title page.
41. 4 Nephi 19-20.
42. 4 Nephi 21.
43. 4 Nephi 24-26.
44. 4 Nephi 46.
45. 4 Nephi 47.
46. 4 Nephi 48-49.
47. Mormon 1:2-4.

The Seer

Carefully, so that he would not skyline himself, the man who had once been known as a prophet and a seer paused and looked around. He stood on a low ridge that was loose with shale, and his only cover was dogwood and hemlock. Yet it was enough, and he knew that if he was careful, he would remain unseen. None of this was conscious, really, for he had been running, almost hiding, for more years than he could remember, so many years that it had become very much second nature to him.

Before him the valley opened quickly, a lovely valley of wide, flat lands broken only occasionally by low finger-like hills. They seemed to stretch on and on, gray and brown and yellow and red up close, but fading with distance to the blues and purples that so moved him each time he gazed upon them. These small hills seemed almost to march in cadence into the distance, step after step, and they made him think of his own journey, a journey that seemed to be taking forever.

Snow had dusted the tops of these hills the night before, an early November snow, and though his breath still hung in the frosty morning air, the clouds had vanished and the sky above him was clear and blue. He was thankful for the fair weather, for it was pleasant and allowed him to continue moving. Still, whatever the weather was, it wouldn't have mattered. In fact, very little seemed to matter anymore except that he place one foot before the other and remain, always and forever, unseen.

Only—he was so lonely, so eternally lonely! Would that never end? Would there never come a time when he could be with people again, when he could talk and laugh and listen and learn and teach? Would there never again be a time when he would feel the warmth of another human near him, another human whom he could trust? Oh, how much longer could he go on, could he endure?

He thought then of his father, recalling him as he stood at the head of his army, and recalling him too as he lay gasping for breath and dying, the victim of an enemy's deadly blow. True, his years had been many, but his strength had been like that of a young man. So too had his enthusiasm for life, though he had despaired of ever seeing his people return to righteousness. Still, because of his love for them, his father had agreed to their pleas to lead them into battle, knowing full well that victory was hopeless.

The man thought of that, saw his father clearly in his mind, and realized instantly that the most vivid picture he had in his memory was not of the old man's death, but of a candle-lit room in a cave, where his father, seated across from him, was speaking.

Many things his father had told him when he was a child, of history and revelation, of good and evil, and of his own future. But the words that remained most clear, the words his mind always came back to, were his father's fervent testimony of the path of living he had chosen.

"My son," the elderly man had solemnly declared while the flickering light from the candle reflected brightly from his deep-set eyes, "long years ago I gave my life to the Lord. He accepted it, and has blessed me greatly. Yet for those blessings I have paid a price, large in ways and yet, according to the words of the great King Benjamin, very insignificant. That price has been loneliness. In the course of my life, few have followed that path, and even fewer have understood. It has been a lofty but lonely way.

"You also, my son, must choose. Along the broad way to destruction flock many people, crowded together and rushing heedlessly downward, their ears filled with the noise from bolstering each other in their sins. The higher way, which leads upward, is born of commitment, courage, and a love of God. But because it requires effort, few make the climb. Because the way is silent and lonely, few have the courage to follow. My son, may God grant that you will do so."

The man, recalling those words, missed his father more than ever; he remembered the love shown him on that same day when he had been held in his father's arms, and once again he felt the old lonely ache in his heart.

For thirty-six years he had climbed as his father had counseled him to do. It had indeed been lonely and difficult, but he had faced it squarely. The problem was that it never seemed to end. Again and again he had prepared to die, and again and again he had lived on. His wandering seemed so pointless, and he had become so discouraged and so very tired.

Dear God of my fathers, he cried silently as he stared down into the empty valley that stretched away before him, *how long must this go on, this emptiness that has been my life these many years?*

He thought then of the woman, the one who had come to his aid in the spring some ten years past. She was only the fourth person he had spoken with in all that time, and she was the first of her race and gender.

He had fallen that day. Somehow the weight of his pack had shifted and had thrown him off balance, and because he was not so young as he had once been, nor as strong, he had lost his footing and had tumbled headlong from the rocks through which he had been making his way.

Sometime later, hours perhaps, or maybe even days, he had felt a hand on his head. It had been warm and soothing, and his heart had leaped with hope.

Opening his eyes he had seen her, leaning over him, concern and compassion written on her face, and he had wondered, briefly, if he had died. Almost instantly, however, he had known otherwise, and he had lain still as she had ministered to him and cared for his wounds.

At first their conversation had been awkward, for it had been so long since he had spoken with anyone, and the hunt for him had been so intense that he had dared trust no one. Yet at once it had been obvious that in spite of her background, she bore him no malice. She carried none of the hatred and anger of her people, and within hours they had both relaxed, and he had felt strangely close to her, sharing much of his travels and of the things he had seen.

Perhaps, he had thought then, *perhaps she is not as the others. Perhaps I may share with her the great gift I have been given, and the eyes of her understanding will be opened. Perhaps—*

Only then, once he had removed his pack and had shown her what he carried, once he had opened his heart and had declared to her some of the things he had known to be true regarding both her people and his own, had he learned how far afield his hopes had been.

The woman had said nothing, had not even moved. But her eyes, her eyes that had been so filled with gentleness, suddenly showed only horror and pity, and he had realized once more that too much had changed, too much had been lost. Suddenly she thought of him as evil, as insane. Even to such a good person as her had the terrible damage been done. Never again, he understood then, would he be able to share!

And so, with a long look back at her sorrowing eyes, he had walked away, knowing full well the pain of loneliness that would follow, and knowing too that there was no choice at all in his decision.

Dear God above, he silently prayed as he thought of the woman, *is there no one left? No one but me who knows Thee, who loves Thee? If so, then why am I here? Of what value is a life alone? The face of that woman haunts me, not so much be-*

*cause I long for companionship, though I do, but because she did
not have ears to hear the way of life, the way of joy eternal.*

*Father, if there are no others who can know, then why must
I tarry? Of what value is a life such as my own? Why, oh why
dost Thou cause me to remain?*

Ah, if only that woman could have understood—

Pushing thoughts of the woman from his mind, the
man again looked carefully around, saw no sign of anyone else, and moved at last from the shelter of the trees.
He feared, though not at all for himself. As far as that
was concerned, he longed for the peace of death. He
feared only for the safety of his pack, for the safety of the
precious things he carried there.

Father, he pleaded silently, *wouldst Thou give me the
strength and wisdom to preserve these things I carry? And give
me, please, an understanding of why Thou hast led me in this direction.*

Farther down the hill, almost at the bottom, the man
paused in a small cove to rest. There was water there, a
clear cold spring, and as he saw it he was reminded of
another place, far away to the west. In that place there
was also water, a great deal of it, gushing forth from
many close-knit springs in a similar cove at the bottom of
a much higher mountain. With its sweet and icy coldness,
the man had once quenched his mighty thirst.

How he had loved it there in that lonely valley, and
how much the Lord had shown him in vision of the long
years ahead and of the final crowning glory of a temple
to the Most High that would one day be built on a hill
near there. Oh, if only he could have lived then, when
there would be such strength, when others too would
know and understand—

But he hadn't been! He lived now, alone, surrounded
by hatred so great that even from that place, that lonely
peaceful valley, he had finally been driven. He was a
hunted man, then and now, hounded always, trailed
constantly, a fugitive from the injustice of those who
feared him and sought his destruction.

Munching on a few tender shoots of watercress,

which even at that late date were still tasty and not strong,
the man stood again and looked around.

The sun was already splashing golden against the
hillside just above him, melting the light dusting of snow
that had fallen, dappling the rocks and making the few
remaining leaves of the birch and the maples even more
brilliant. The air was heavy with the smell of wet earth,
and the music of the water as if flowed and swirled past
him caused him to feel again his old sense of awe and
gratitude.

It is so beautiful, his heart sang out to his God, *this world
that Thou hast created. In places such as this my soul sings with
praise and joy, and I marvel at the loveliness and vastness of Thy
handiwork. Father, as Thou hast made of this land a place of
beauty, do Thou also with the life of this Thy servant. Help me to
have patience, to understand that Thy wisdom surpasseth all
things, and that my life, my lonely life, is according to Thy will.*

Do with me as seemeth to Thee good, and I will be content.

All morning the man moved east through the grass-
filled valley, brown now with the coming winter. His
mood was melancholy, more so than it had been in
months. Yet there was also a strange sense of destiny
with him, a feeling that maybe he had seen this valley before, though he felt certain that he hadn't.

The sun was almost straight above him when the man
thought again of his wife, his beloved and long-departed
companion of eternity. It was not often that he allowed
himself to think of her, for the memories were as painful
as they were sweet. But this day they came, unbidden,
brought on by the sound of a lark, a sound that she had
loved dearly, and he was unable to hold his memories
away.

Her fair-skinned face seemed to float in the air before him, not sought but welcome. How he loved her,
and how he longed to be with her, to hear her musical
laughter, to feel the tender touch of her fingers on his
face, to see her eyes light up with joy and understanding
as he explained to her an eternal pearl of wisdom or
knowledge that the Lord in his mercy had revealed. He
missed her so much that he could not begin to describe it,

even to himself, and all of the years since her death had
not caused the loneliness to be less.

He missed too his sons and his daughters, for he had
loved them more than life itself. How he had delighted
in them, those young children, in their joys and sorrows,
in their triumphs and even in their failures.

His sons had been growing so tall, so straight and so
strong. They were fighters all, but their hearts had been
pure too, and they were all anxious to follow in the ways
of their father, the ways of love and righteousness that
had also been the ways of his own father.

His daughters, fair-skinned and dark-haired like
their mother, were like her too in their compassion. And,
he recalled, grinning, they had been like her in temper-
ament as well, kind and gentle unless aroused by cruelty
or evil, and then fierce in their opposition to it.

The man smiled again, remembering a day when
neighboring children had tormented and nearly killed a
small animal. His eldest daughter, seeing their act of
cruelty, had flown at them with a stick and, alone, had
driven all of them off. Then she had taken the animal
and nursed it back to health, earning forever her father's
devotion for her courage and tenderness, and earning
forever his love and respect.

Tears welled up in the man's eyes, tears of loneliness
and sorrow because those he loved were gone, murdered
as they had slept that long-ago night. He had been away
on an errand of mercy, and they had slept peacefully,
unaware, unafraid—

Now, he thought as he wiped at his eyes, those lovely
children would never grow to manhood, to womanhood.
They would never, at least in mortality, know the joys of
a love for an eternal companion, never feel the weight of
child of their own against their breast or upon their
knee, never understand—

"Oh Father," he whispered, "I know that they are
happy with Thee, and I do not mean to murmur. Yet
how I would that they had been given a chance—just a
chance—"

Ahead of the man a hill loomed up, a steep hill that

seemed higher than the others around it. Stopping, he wiped the tears from his tired old eyes and then gazed up through the barren trees and brush to the summit, reluctant to climb it and yet feeling, somehow, that he should.

Glancing around once more he made certain that he was alone, though actually he hadn't needed to look. Over the years he had developed a sixth sense that told him when others were near, a sense that thus far had never failed. And that too had been a direct blessing, a promise made him by both the resurrected Lord and the only three others of his people he had seen in over thirty years of wandering.

The three and their Master, Jesus Christ, had visited him, both together and singly, only occasionally. Yet their visits had come at crucial times, and their love, wisdom, and testimonies had supported him and had given him the strength he had needed to carry on when all had seemed so hopeless. Years had passed, however, since he had seen the Lord or the three, and once more he wondered how much longer he could continue in such absolute solitude.

Slowly the man began the climb before him, and as he did he wondered at himself and at the urgency he was suddenly feeling. Within him was the knowledge that he should be moving on, for it was late in the year and he needed to be far to the south, where the sun warmed the aching in his joints and where the cold did not gnaw so ferociously at his tired and ancient body. Yet something was drawing him up that hill, something that had been pulling at him for days as he had journeyed eastward—

Once on top, the man who had been known as a prophet and seer stopped and stared, experiencing again the sense of something almost remembered, the sense of a place once seen before, but not.

Feeling more lonely than he could ever remember, he gazed out into the valley, hoping to see some sign of human habitation, some sign even of the presence of those who called themselves his enemies.

How he missed his people. How he longed, despite their hatred of him, to go to them, to sit with them and break bread, and to share with them the great things the Lord had placed within his heart. Only he couldn't, not yet, not so long as their hatred burned as deeply as it did.

The quiet of the early afternoon was profound and intense. Not a bird sang, not an insect whirred or buzzed, not an animal moved. Across the valley the low hills marched solemnly back in the direction he had come, blue and hazy and lovely in their panoramic splendor. Against his face the afternoon sun felt warm, but suddenly a wind sprang up behind him, blowing chill against his neck, and the man sensed again the nearness of the coming winter.

Father, he thought as he pulled his fur more tightly around his shoulders, *each year the winter comes with greater speed. I awakened this morning and found snow clinging to the hills, eating away the final days of summer in much the same manner that time has eaten away the days of my life.*

Above me are geese in V-shaped flight, their cries echoing on the wind as they race before the cold. They have the urge for going, and I who am not allowed to declare the words of truth and life to my brethren whom I love, I who am not allowed to know the companionship of others, I also have the urge to leave.

May I not soon know the reasons—

Suddenly the man was aware that something before him was changing. As he watched with mounting excitement and not a little reverence he saw the trees ahead open a little, and he knew without doubt that he was seeing again—seeing—

Quickly he stepped forward, off the brow of the hill, down the slope, pulling from his pack the silver bow his father had fashioned, fitting it hastily into his armor, setting the stones, looking into and through them, seeing—

They were opening wide now, the barren trees before him, and it was also fall where the vision showed, only earlier, and the trees were much different and hardly as thick. Their leaves, down through that long vista of time, were only just beginnig to pick up a little autumn color, and the man guessed as he gazed with the eyes of his spirit into the two stones that it was late September that he was seeing.

It was still and noonday in the vision before him, and as he watched intently he saw a young boy move upward along the slope, pausing now and then, looking. The man wondered at that, and then he saw the boy suddenly stop and gaze upward, almost toward him. The boy's face lighted, and the man was shocked at how familiar the young man seemed. Only how, when—

"Father," he whispered as he watched, "the face of this youth seems familiar, and yet I know him not. Who is he, and what has he to do with me? He is so young, so unlearned, so guileless, and yet I sense, I sense—

Straight toward him the boy in the vision came, straight toward a low rock that lay between both of them, rounded at the top and spreading wide at its base. It wasn't the rock, however, that the boy sought. It was something else, something that was obviously much more important.

And then the man smiled radiantly, for he knew, and at last he also understood.

"Ah," he said, still whispering in prayer, "so this is he. I have wondered, and yet all along I have felt that I would know. I see now that he is indeed innocent, for I perceive that Thou hast directed his course since birth.

"Father, I am honored that Thou hast shown me this youth whom Thou wilt raise up, and I am honored too that Thou hast brought me here, to the spot where the words of my soul, and the voices of my people, will rise from the dust to mingle with the voice of this lad, who will one day be a mighty prophet unto Thee."

For an instant longer the man watched, memorizing the boy's face, seeing there the courage and conviction and righteousness and desire, as well as the uncertainty and doubt, that filled the boy's heart. The man knew that he would see him again, but still he watched until the vision closed and he was alone once more. Then quickly, after another look at the stone that lay partially buried in the earth before him, the man sat down, removed from his pack the priceless treasure handed to him by his father, and began with care to write.

Now I, Moroni, he inscribed on the metal plates as he blinked back his tears of gratitude and excitement, *Now I, Moroni, write somewhat as seemeth me good; (for) I soon go to rest in the paradise of my God.*

And I write unto my brethren . . .

And I seal up these records, after I have spoken a few words by way of exhortation unto you . . .

And when ye shall receive these things . . .

From the Book of Moroni we discover that . . .

Moroni, the final prophet to record his testimony on the plates that became, after translation by Joseph Smith, Jr., the Book of Mormon, was probably the most lonely of all ancient American prophets. His father, the prophet Mormon, called his son to him sometime before A.D. 385[1] and gave to him the ancient records he had been keeping. He then commanded Moroni to write upon them and to seal them up when he was finished.[2] Shortly thereafter Mormon was killed, probably in the great battle of Cumorah.[3]

From then until he finally buried the records for the last time in A.D. 421, Moroni was essentially alone. He does tell us that he was acquainted with the three Nephite disciples who had been allowed to tarry,[4] and he informs us as well that he had met Jesus Christ and had spoken with him face to face.[5] Other than that, however, his record indicates that he was alone for the last thirty-six years of his life.[6]

He tells us that he was very lonely.[7] He explains that he was always in hiding from the Lamanites who thirsted for his blood,[8] and the length of time he remained alive seems to have been a surprise and a puzzlement to him.[9] Apparently he thought he would die more than once, and he ended his record each of those times.[10] When he continued to live, he occupied himself with making more plates[11] and abridging the twenty-four gold plates of the Jaradite prophet Ether.[12] That completed, he transcribed one lecture and two important letters from his father Mormon,[13] added vital information concerning Christ's calling of the twelve disciples,[14] elaborated on doctrines concerning priesthood ordinations and the administration of the sacrament,[15] and discussed proper Church discipline and procedure.[16] He also wrote a direct and pointed letter to the Latter-day translator of the plates, Joseph Smith, wherein he warned him against translating the sealed portion of his plates.[17] Finally, in what was indeed his farewell message, he taught of gifts of the Spirit,[18] made several promises by the power of the priesthood,[19] and concluded with his own personal and powerful testimony.[20]

In the midst of his loneliness, Moroni developed great spirituality, and the Lord allowed him to spend much time enwrapped in visions, seeing into the future.[21]

To do this, Moroni apparently used, at least to a certain extent, two stones that the Lord had originally given to the Brother of Jared when they spoke face to face on the mount[22] and which were called Urim and Thummim.[23] The Nephites had access to them at least from the time of King Mosiah,[24] and, as Ammon explained, their use constituted the calling of a seer, a prophet, and a revelator.[25] He also explained that a seer can know of things past, things that are to come, hidden things, and unknown things that otherwise could never be known.[26] Moroni also had these interpreters, used them, and tells us that he was commanded to seal them up with the sacred records.[27]

What Moroni saw of the future through the two sacred stones gave him comfort as well as distress, and he forcefully counseled future members of Christ's church concerning weaknesses they would have, which the Lord had shown him in just such a vision or visions.[28]

Finally, however, some event or whispering of the Spirit gave him to know that his mission was nearly over.[29] Therefore he took the plates and wrote upon them for the last time, exhorting future readers to righteousness and declaring to them his final testimony.[30]

With that, his record ends, and we hear no more from him until the night of September 21, 1823, when he appeared in glory to the young Joseph Smith,[31] who had been called and foreordained to bring Moroni's buried records forth from the earth for the salvation of God's children.

Truly Moroni the prophet and seer, for the good of us all, chose the lofty and lonely way of living.

1. Mormon 7, footnote.
2. Mormon 8:1, 3-4; Moroni 9:24.
3. Mormon 8:2-3.
4. Mormon 8:10-11 (see "The Witness" story and "Discovery" note and "The Conference" story and "Discovery" note in this volume for more information on the three Nephite disciples).
5. Ether 12:39.
6. Moroni 10:1.
7. Mormon 8:5.
8. Moroni 1:3.
9. Moroni 1:1, 4.
10. Mormon 8:5-6 (four hundred years had now passed since Christ's birth) Mormon 8:13; Moroni 1:1-4 (written between A.D. 400 and A.D. 421).
11. Mormon 8:5 (Moroni explains here that he has no more plates nor ore with which to make them; yet soon he is abridging the entire record of Ether, plus writing more on his own. Apparently he not only found ore, but also found the way to work it into plates.).
12. Ether 1:2.
13. Moroni 7, 8, 9.
14. Moroni 2.
15. Moroni 3, 4, 5.
16. Moroni 6.
17. Ether 5:1-6.
18. Moroni 10:8-18.
19. Moroni 10:4-5, 7, 19, 21, 24-28.
20. Moroni 10:29-34.
21. Mormon 8:34-35.
22. Doctrine and Covenants 17:1.
23. Doctrine and Covenants 10:1.
24. Mosiah 8:13.
25. Mosiah 8:16.
26. Mosiah 8:17.
27. Ether 4:5-6.
28. Mormon 8:36-41.
29. Moroni 10:34.
30. Moroni 10:1-34.
31. Joseph Smith—History 1:29-34.